Canada's Water:
For Sale?

Canada's Water:
For Sale?

Richard C. Bocking

James Lewis & Samuel, Publishers
Toronto
1972

ISBN   0-88862-028-4 (cloth)
ISBN   0-88862-044-6 (paper)
Library of Congress card catalogue No: 72-90591

Cover design by Lynn Campbell
Cover photograph by John de Visser

James Lewis & Samuel, Publishers
35 Britain Street
Toronto
Canada

Printed and bound in Canada

Table of Contents

For Winnifred

Introduction

This book began as a film. In 1969, the Canadian Broadcasting Corporation agreed to a proposal of mine for a television program concerning the question of export of Canadian water to the United States. It appeared on the CBC network in the fall of 1970, as a program in the "Tuesday Night" series, under the title "Canada's Water — For Sale?"*

Research on the program was begun with a number of preconceptions. First, of course, I accepted as fact that a shortage of water in the United States was approaching the critical stage, and that the U.S. would need to look to Canada for help. Another assumption was that Canada had plenty of water, and could quite possibly give consideration to such a proposition. But two important questions had to be faced: what would such an arrangement mean to the independence of Canada, and what effect would massive water diversions have on the environment of Canada?

In journalism, whether for television or other media, it often turns out that preconceptions existing when work begins on a project are confirmed by initial research, but turn out to be quite incorrect as research probes deeper. So it was with this program. The superficially strong evidence of U.S. "need" for more water evaporated with in-depth study. The whole field of water development, long viewed as the embodiment of man's mastery over nature for the good of society, turned out to be largely a story of political manipulation of mind-boggling proportions. Amazing engineering work is frequently justified by a strange kind of economics that is remarkable for its lack of relationship to reality. Environmental ramifications of massive water developments are only now being spelled out in their truly enormous proportions.

*This program has been turned into a colour film which is available from the Visual Education Centre, 115 Berkeley Street, Toronto 2A. The full version of the program is 55 minutes long; a shortened version which runs for 21 minutes is also available.

It soon became evident that a television program on this subject could only create a general awareness about it, and that relatively full development of the question could come only from book-length treatment. Even the medium of this book has not allowed for a full discussion of all aspects of the water development and export questions, and I regret, for instance, that it was not possible to develop a complete analysis of the James Bay project in Quebec, or of the water development recommendations of the B.C. Energy Board, which were released after the book was in press. It is hoped, however, that the book will provide a basic understanding of some of the principles and issues involved in any water development project, whether international or domestic, so that the reader will feel more able to assess for himself the continuing stream of water development projects that are being promoted by governments, hydro electric authorities, and those who stand to gain from such projects in one way or another.

The scope of this book is intended to be broader than its title might indicate. It is clear that the ramifications of water development projects currently underway or proposed within Canada's borders deserve immediate and careful reconsideration by the people of Canada. So, while parts of the book relate almost solely to the water export issue, most of it is concerned with water development generally, whether within Canada or involving the export of water or power.

The first three chapters consider the nature of the water "crisis" in the U.S., the reality of the often-expressed need for Canadian water south of the border, and the sources of pressures that may lead to international water diversion. Chapters 4-8 consider the impact of water development on man and the environment and examine the institutions and attitudes that create the pressures for such development. The strange world of water economics is explored in some detail, and alternative ways of approaching water shortages, whether real or imaginary, are suggested.

The final two chapters discuss directions in which Canadian water policy might evolve as a consequence of the basic philosophy that emerges from a broad examination of water development. It is difficult to define the relationship of Canadian identity to the water resources of the nation, but an attempt at this has been made and it is the subject of the final chapter of the book.   R.C.B.

North Vancouver, B.C.   September 1972

Acknowledgements

This book could never have been written without the prior production of the CBC television program of the same name, and I wish to express my deep appreciation to the Canadian Broadcasting Corporation and those officials of the Corporation who authorized the project and were generous in their encouragement. These include, particularly, Robert Patchell, William Harcourt, Raymond Whitehouse and Knowlton Nash. I should note that while the television program was a relatively objective report on the issues involved, the book on the contrary is highly subjective. It summarizes the conclusions I reached after much research, and does not attempt to put forth representative views on all sides of each aspect of the question.

A great many people contributed ideas and help in the preparation of this book and the film that preceeded it, and I mention names with much trepidation, knowing that important contributors will be missed. In the references section at the end of the book I have listed many of those with whom I have discussed water developments. Interviews were filmed with most of them. A few names stand out, however, as having influenced major aspects of the book. The basic philosophy of water development in the book has been strongly influenced by Gilbert White of the University of Colorado, who is known around the world for his enlightened approach to the subject of water development. In developing an approach to the economics of water development I was particularly influenced by John Krutilla and Charles Howe of Resources for the Future, Inc., in Washington D.C., Larratt Higgins of Ontario Hydro, James A. Crutchfield of the University of Washington in Seattle, Michael Goldberg of the University of British Columbia, and William Martin of the University of Arizona. Robert Newbury of the University of Manitoba and Luna B. Leopold of the U.S. Geological Service helped me to acquire an understanding of the nature of river systems, while the approach taken to an understanding of ecological aspects of water development owes much to Donald Chant of the University of Toronto, Dennis McDonald of the Alberta Fish and Game Branch, and C. S. Holling of the University of British Columbia. David Brower of Friends of the Earth and Stewart Brandborg of the Wilderness Society helped deepen my understanding of the losses inherent in the manipulation of our finest natural landscapes through water development.

Particular help and encouragement over an extended period of time was provided by Derrick Sewell of the University of Victoria and Frank Quinn of the Department of the Environment in Ottawa, Dixon Thompson of the Science Council of Canada and Robert Newbury of the University of Manitoba. Frank Quinn and Derrick Sewell read parts of the manuscript and offered valued suggestions for its improvement, but of course neither they nor any of the others mentioned above, nor any of those consulted during the preparation of the book, are in any way responsible for the errors or omissions or inadequacies of this book. For all of these I am solely responsible.

Finally, I wish to express my deep appreciation to my wife and family for their acceptance of the sacrifices this book entailed for them. I would like in particular to thank my son, Douglas, who typed the final manuscript, and most important of all, express my deep appreciation to my wife, without whose patience and encouragement the book could not have been written.

Chapter 1
Does the U.S. need Canadian Water?

Across the desert near Phoenix, Arizona, a deep crevass makes its jagged way toward a nearby suburb. Several feet wide, it disappears into blackness in many places. Visitors are told that it is hundreds of feet deep, that it is just one of many such fissures in the Salt River Valley of Central Arizona, and that it results from a water shortage so desperate that the ground is settling into the cavities caused by excessive pumping of the water which lies under the valley.

This great split in the earth is shown to visitors from other parts of the continent to emphasize the thirst of the southwestern United States. The point is emphasized for Canadians, and for visitors from the Pacific Northwest states of Washington and Oregon. For these regions have water resources that many Americans consider necessary to the growth and well being of the Southwest—the fastest growing section of the United States.

The point has been well made. In recent years, a stream of books, magazine and newspaper articles, and political pronouncements have proclaimed "The Water Crisis" one of the most serious problems to be faced by Americans in the very near future. U.S. Senator Frank Moss of Utah summarized much of this point of view in his 1967 book *The Water Crisis*, and U.S. Congressman Jim Wright added his voice in a book called *The Coming Water Famine*. Governor Ronald Reagan of California and Governor Jack Williams of Arizona have made it clear that they are anxious to talk to anyone who might have surplus water available for diversion south. Governor Tom McCall of Oregon has called for immediate negotiation with Canada to determine what surplus Canadian water could be diverted south of the border.

To ensure that the message gets across, writers and broadcasters, and others interested in water resources from comparatively water-rich regions of the continent have been guests of the various lobbies and organizations in the United States dedicated to the importation of water into those areas. Typical was a tour in 1970 organized by the Colorado River

Association and the Central Arizona Project Association. The message was clear, and duly reported in newspapers throughout those areas of the United States and Canada usually considered to have surplus water flowing to the sea. It read: "We're dry, we're soon going to be in desperate need of water, we need your help."

The point is seldom questioned in Canada. Politicians of all parties assume that the American need for more water is great and growing. Many Canadian writers, even nationalistic ones such as Walter Stewart of *Maclean's* magazine, accept as fact that a need exists, that Canada will eventually have to sell water to the United States, and that Canadians must evolve a policy now that will protect Canada's interests when such a deal eventually is made. So perceptive a writer as Bob Hunter of the Vancouver *Sun* describes the desperate nature of the American water predicament in terms of lowered water tables and deeper wells, thousands of acres and whole towns abandoned in some states as a result of water shortages.

Donald Waterfield, whose book *Continental Waterboy* documents the battle of residents of the Columbia Valley to save their land from flooding by the dams built under the Columbia River Treaty, concedes that enormous water transfers from Canada to the United States will be "inevitable," unless the American population is stabilized. Horrifying as he considers it to be, Waterfield accepts the disastrous nature of the water situation in the United States, and the inability of Canada to withstand the demands of a mighty neighbour as it looks northward for more water.

In the face of all this, it is not surprising to find some Canadians reacting as did one Vancouver housewife: "If our neighbours are thirsty, how can we possibly deny them some of the water that we don't really need ourselves?"

The attitudes of Canadians generally, of politicians, and of writers and broadcasters, have been shaped in response to a mainly unquestioning acceptance of the fact of a great and growing need for more water in the United States. And so before considering the political, economic, social, and ecological implications of water export to the United States, and indeed of water development generally, it's vital that the American need for more water be carefully examined.

Little heard in Canada, and ignored as much as possible in the United States, there is a growing body of responsible opinion in the U.S. that "The Water Crisis" may not be so real as it is usually considered to be. In 1966, a prestigious committee of some of the best-known U.S. water resource experts stated in a report issued by the National Academy of Sciences and the National Research Council: "This report is not prompted by a national water shortage, for there is no nationwide shortage and no imminent danger of one."

The chairman of the committee that produced the report was Dr. Gilbert F. White of the University of Colorado. Dr. White is one of the world's most respected authorities in the field of water resources and arid lands. In a 1970 interview, he said: "There is no shortage of water in the United States that is seriously impeding the economic growth of the country. In the Eastern States, clearly there is no shortage of water so far as growth of urban areas or industry is concerned. There are problems of quality of water, of deterioration of water, but not of quantity. In the Western States, there is no shortage of water for urban or industrial growth. Conceivably, we are short of water if we want to greatly expand irrigation agriculture, but whether or not we should do this is a grave question of national policy."

The eastern half of the United States is normally a well watered area, averaging from 40 to 50 inches of rainfall a year and served by a great many streams of remarkably even flow. But it was in the northeastern states during the five year period from 1961 to 1966 that a water shortage focussed attention upon what has become known as "The Water Crisis". It was the most severe drought experienced in the region in historical times. Although low rainfall had been experienced in the eighteen nineties, the effect then was not particularly severe since populations were much lower and the use per person much less.

"Save water, shower with a friend" was a slogan coined at the time, but the reality of the situation saw New York restaurants forbidden to serve drinking water unless specifically requested to do so; swimming pools and fountains were shut down; car washing and lawn sprinkling prohibited. Air conditioning was limited in commercial buildings. Reservoirs were drawn down far below their capacity. Low flows in many streams were insufficient to flush away the sewage dumped into them, and pollution became a serious problem.

But there is another side to the story. Dr. Derrick Sewell is an economist and geographer at the University of Victoria, author of eight books on resource economics and one of the continent's authorities in the field of water resources. Says Dr. Sewell: "It seems to me that there is no real water shortage in many of these areas if you take into account the amount of waste that does occur in such regions. For example, if you look at cities in the American Northeast, in many of them as much as 20 to 30 per cent of the water leaks out of the water system before it reaches the customer. Obviously it would be very hard to say that there is a water shortage when wastage on that scale does occur."

The comparison is often made that while the 7 million people of London, England use about 420 million gallons of water daily, New York manages to waste 300 million gallons each day. This appalling figure is a total of losses from the city's water mains, and of wastage by the 8 million citizens of the city. The waste can be laid at the door of civic politicians, according to many critics. There is no incentive for citizens to avoid wasting water because it is so cheap.

Simply installing meters would eliminate a great deal of wastage, and this has been recommended many times, but apparently has not been considered politically palatable. In addition, Dr. Sewell suggests: "The price of water is typically much lower than the cost of supplying it, and certainly much lower than the price that ought to be paid in terms of its value. So it seems to me that if you raised the price of water people would probably be less prone to waste it to the extent they do now". Most of the water consumed in the United States is sold at prices below full cost. Economist Dr. James A. Crutchfield of the University of Washington contends that: "A water crisis could be created anywhere in the nation by making it cheap enough."

Probably the greatest paradox in the New York problem is in fact symptomatic of the water problem across the continent. The Hudson River, one of the great streams of North America, flows right by the city. It has however become so polluted that it cannot be used as a water supply. Cleaning it up is quite possible technically, but apparently it is politically difficult. And so the water problem in the well-watered eastern half of the continent is not one of shortages, but of bad management that can certainly be overcome through applying modern water management principles in the regions involved. There is no way in which water importation could be considered a rational solution to these local problems.

West of the Mississippi River, however, the problem is a much more complex one, and it is for that part of the United

States that most, although not all, Canadian water export schemes are put forth.

More than 90 per cent of the water used in the arid southwestern states is devoted to irrigated agriculture. Some of that is, of course, used to grow hot weather crops that cannot be produced elsewhere; citrus fruits, dates, and vegetables that arrive fresh on the tables of a continent largely gripped by cold weather during the winter months. But most of the water is used to grow cotton, a surplus and subsidized commodity; and low value crops such as alfalfa, barley and grain sorghum, crops which can be grown elsewhere and which in any case aren't in short supply.

"The Southwest talks so often about the need for water for the thirsty millions in Southern California and so on, but they're not really talking about that at all," says Dr. Crutchfield. "It is really for the continued expansion of irrigated agriculture that the need, so called, for inter-basin transfers to supplement the shrinking supplies in the Southwest really arises."

Under various government programs, about 56 million acres of American farm land has been withdrawn from production in an effort to keep agricultural surpluses from becoming overwhelming. Even greater surplus problems appear imminent with the likelihood of reduced government support for cotton growers. This highly subsidized crop is facing reduced demand each year as artificial fibres replace it in many uses, and it cannot be grown without government help. Large acreages used to produce cotton are expected to be diverted to other crops, particularly the higher value fruits and vegetables. Agricultural economists such as Dr. David Seckler of the University of California at Berkeley expect this increased production to push down the prices of these crops, to the disadvantage of the agricultural industry generally.

Dr. Charles Howe and Dr. William Easter in a recent book published by Resources for the Future in Washington, D.C. estimate that between 5 and 17 million acres of farm land in other areas of the United States were forced out of production by new irrigated land between 1944 and 1964. Subsidized irrigation in the west made cheaper production of some crops possible, pushing out of production land that normally grew those crops in other regions, principally the southern U.S.

This contributed to the movement of unemployed farm

workers into the cities, usually the ghetto areas. The social costs are incalculable, and the actual costs to the American taxpayer have been enormous.

One of the best illustrations of the strange relationships that have developed in irrigated agriculture in the United States is this: in the 171 counties containing most of the 8 million acres irrigated by Bureau of Reclamation projects to 1965, over 3 million acres were retired from production to reduce surpluses. This was precisely the amount of land the Bureau had brought into production in these same areas during the preceding 20 years.

From all of this, Dr. William E. Martin and Dr. Robert A. Young, agricultural economists at the University of Arizona, conclude: "Although economic growth in the west may originally have been based on a liberal water supply, additional water is no longer necessary (at least in the foreseeable future) and may in fact be 'detrimental to our health!' "

Less than 10 per cent of the water consumed in the southwestern States is used in the homes of its people and by industry. Dr. Crutchfield suggests that diverting as little as ten per cent of the water now used to grow low value crops in the irrigated areas of these states would double the water available for all other uses. There would be very little cost in reduced agricultural production, since low value products would be the crops reduced in acreage. "The impact on southwestern agriculture would be largely in the direction of producing higher valued crops using much more efficient irrigation techniques than they now bother to use—no deserts are going to be created." This sort of thing is indeed happening in Arizona, where Phoenix is spreading over the irrigated lands of the Salt River Valley, and the water used for irrigation now is available for domestic and industrial use. Since these uses are of much greater economic importance to an area than is agriculture, the overall effect on the economy is a beneficial one.

In Arizona, for instance, half of all the water used grows comparatively low value grain and forage crops, and provides a return of about 16 dollars per acre foot of water used. The same amount of water used in manufacturing in the state brings a return of more than 80,000 dollars per acre foot. Another view of the same situation reveals that although grains and forage crop use about 54% of all the water consumed in Arizona, these crops contribute only

1.5% of the income of the entire state economy.

In terms of the United States as a whole, or any particular state, it becomes clear that dropping water tables and shrinking agricultural areas have no serious economic effect. But the individual farm corporation (family farms have almost vanished from the Southwest) that is directly affected, with water costs rising due to the increased expense of pumping, might be expected to view the situation differently. The case is often made that the farms of Arizona, for instance, are faced with a simple alternative — import more water or face disaster.

Any large scale importation of water into the dry areas of the Southwest would cost a minimum of $50 to $60 an acre foot (an acre foot is the amount of water that would cover an acre to a depth of one foot) and would likely range much higher, since farmers at present pay rates ranging from just over 2 dollars per acre foot in the Imperial Valley, to a maximum of 7 or 8 dollars per acre foot for water pumped from beneath the Arizona desert. It is obvious that enormous subsidies will be required to provide this water at a price that will make it useful to farmers.

Dr. W. Martin and Dr. R. Young have analyzed the effect that imported water would have on the farm corporations of the state, and have found that water costing more than $3 or $4 at the main canal would actually reduce the income of farmers and cause the land to be devalued, since their present water is less expensive. Yet water to be imported to the Phoenix-Tucson areas by the Central Arizona Project will cost farmers $10 at the main canal and of course that is far below cost. To bring the water right to the farm would bring the total cost to nearly $18 per acre foot. That's very expensive water, much more costly than that presently and for long into the future available through existing irrigation systems in Arizona. In the Phoenix area, for example, farmers pay $1.50 per acre foot for water supplied by the Salt River Valley irrigation project.

Farmers do have serious problems of markets and rising costs. Increasing the costs of water through massive subsidized importation schemes hardly seems the way to help them, particularly when there is enough underground water available at economic costs to last even at present rates of withdrawal for 170 years.

The ominous crack in the ground near Phoenix is related to another fact which is behind the promotion of water importation into Arizona. The water under the desert supplies 4½ million acre feet of water to the state each year. That's 70% of all the water used. But the level of that ground water is dropping 8 to 10 feet each year. The great underground aquifer or water reservoir which accumulated over thousands of years is being pumped out much faster than new water can accumulate in it. Wells must drive deeper each year for a good flow of water. In some places, it no longer is economical to pump the water to the surface for agricultural use, particularly for low value crops, and the land has been abandoned. Everywhere, the cost of bringing it to the surface is rising.

Some southern regions, like the high plains of Texas, are totally dependent on pumped water for the maintenance of agriculture. The water accumulated underground hundreds of thousands of years ago and is being replenished at a very slow rate, certainly far too slowly to offset the unlimited pumping that irrigates five and a half million acres of the region. Before World War II there were about 600 wells pumping on the high plains; now more than 11 thousand wells are causing the water table to drop about ten feet a year, and the people are demanding help.

The help they want is in the form of the Texas Water Plan which would bring water from the Mississippi across the state to "rescue" the high plains. The cost estimates range from 6 to 13 billion dollars.

It is such "rescue" proposals that are often cited in making the case for desperately needed water in the United States. And they must be considered in a somewhat different light from those regions where alternatives are available as water becomes more scarce and expensive. The enormous costs involved in almost all "rescue" projects, would be paid for largely by taxpayers outside of the region affected. As will be shown in chapter 5, Canada could be very much affected by such proposals.

Dr. Gilbert White looks at it this way: "There is nothing inherent in a situation in which people have exhausted the underground water that requires national effort to bail them out. We do not expect to go in and replace coal which the coal miners have taken out of the earth. We do not expect to inject copper into the ground where strip mines have removed it. But we seem to feel that where a farmer has ruthlessly and wantonly exhausted the water that lies beneath his property, taking far more each year than flows in nature, there is some kind of responsibility to replace that water which he has wasted."

The record solidly supports Dr. White. The Bureau of Reclamation, and several state governors, pressed hard for the implementation of controls that would limit pumping of groundwater to an amount reasonably close to that being returned to the natural reservoir. Successive state legislatures refused to do so, reflecting the preference of the farmers that the cost of pumping determine how much would be used. They preferred that economics, rather than law and principles of conservation, control use of underground water supplies.

The fact remains, however, that in the case of the Texas high plains, a whole economy has arisen in which many of the resources and investments are quite immobile and cannot be removed to other areas. The value of the land itself declines to very low levels without water; towns providing services and processing facilities for agriculture would wither and die as the farms gradually go out of business as the water table drops too far for economic pumping. Should water from Canada or anywhere else be brought in at great expense to prevent this?

A careful analysis of this question has been made by Dr. Charles Howe and Dr. William Easter in their Resources for the Future study mentioned earlier. They point out that if the agriculture of the area is phased out gradually, the investment in it and supporting businesses can be written off over a period of time at little financial loss to those involved. It may be that a good case could be made for public payment of the losses that do occur as the water table drops, the costs of moving displaced people to other areas, and the retraining of unemployed workers. The amounts involved should be carefully compared with costs of great water "rescue" projects which would be unquestionably uneconomic even if the agricultural production were needed, which it clearly is not. There are usually many alternatives available other than supplying more water, in situations which at first glance appear to be purely water problems.

Most of the statements of need for more water in the United States are based on projections of probable population, industrial, and agricultural growth in the future. These estimates are almost always made in a most simplistic way, usually by projection of rates of growth of the recent past into the future. This provides a forecast of geometric growth rates in consumption of water (or energy, or automobiles, or refrigerators, or anything else) which in a world of limited resources is questionable, to say the least. Someone has calculated that at the present rate of construction of electrical generating plants, the U.S. would be completely covered with such plants in less than 200 years. At just about the same time, according to someone else's figures, the U.S. would be totally paved with freeways and parking lots at present construction rates. Such projections reduce to ludicrousness suggestions and plans based on a long term continuation of present growth rates. Yet it is on precisely such growth rates that much of the predictions of need are based.

Planners usually avoid confronting the questionable nature of their long-term projections by picking a shorter period of time. Thirty years, or the year 2000, is a currently fashionable period. What is never included in estimates of future needs is the fact that the year 2000 is not a plateau, a goal that will be achieved. Building for such predicted levels of water use will incorporate such a rate of growth in water consumption that the problems of keeping up with requirements in the year 2001 will be far greater than those encountered in supplying the quantities "required" prior to 2000.

Projected requirements are almost always put forth as "meeting needs". Very often, however, they turn out to be self-fulfilling prophecies. If the water is provided, or the power plant is built, or the road constructed, then the water, or the electricity, or the highway will be fully utilized by bringing more land into irrigation, or encouraging an aluminum plant to establish in an area of excess electrical energy. Highways are usually overloaded immediately upon being built, not so much demonstrating the accuracy of those who prophesied their need, but showing the result of starvation of other forms of transportation to provide those roads, and the effect of promotion of investment in industry and suburban development along them.

One indication that the future will not be a projection of the past is already occurring where it was least expected. Southern California is growing at a rate considerably slower than had been predicted and upon which its water planning was based. A 1971 poll indicated that nearly one third of the state's residents considered other regions of their nation as more desirable places to live, and gave overcrowding and pollution as reasons for this feeling. Not long ago it was a rare Californian who considered his state to be anything less than "the promised land". But in the year preceding June 3, 1971, Los Angeles county actually declined in population for the first time in its history.

The basic assumptions underlying American "need" for Canadian water are increasingly questioned in the United States. There is no longer universal acceptance of the need for further growth at any cost, and many Californians are making a concerted effort to slow down development of the state, rather than provide great influxes of new resources such as water in order to allow for massive new surges of growth. The smog generated in southern California and particularly in the Los Angeles area has reached such a stage that on some days school smog warnings are issued, along with the radio news and weather reports. On such days, teachers are not to allow their students outside at recess — the heavy breathing resulting from running and playing will draw too much of the poisonous atmosphere into their lungs. One of the region's foremost experts on the subject, Dr. A. J. Haagen Smit, was outraged at the invitation extended to hold the 1976 Olympic games at Los Angeles. The risk to competitors straining their bodies in the smog of southern California was unacceptable, he was convinced.

Add to this the rate of development of California which sees about 400 acres a day paved over and built upon, and the dimensions of the problem become apparent. Much of the land disappearing under freeways and subdivisions and industrial parks is good agricultural land, some of it producing the finest citrus fruit on the continent. New land being brought under irrigation to replace it is of poorer quality.

Then, of course, there is the simple press of humanity, removing from many the possibility of privacy, of undisturbed green spaces, of a life free of the regimentation that will inevitably accompany the crowding that is becoming a day to day reality.

Conservationist David Brower, President of Friends of the Earth, an international organization centred in San Francisco, insists that pouring more water into southern California would simply aggravate what he considers to be a disaster area. Dr. Paul Ehrlich of Stanford University, author of *The Population Bomb*, states that what is required is a cutting back on the level of demand for water, and for other resources too. He suggests that California is already monstrously over-developed, that a halt must be called, and that a good place to stop would be in the provision of more water. U.S. Representative Jerome Waldie of California has taken up this cause in Congress. "They ought to abolish and outlaw the Chamber of Commerce syndrome through all of California, but particularly in Los Angeles, that growth is good and massive growth is better; that's nonsense in this day and age . . . !"

In Arizona similar problems are being encountered as more people are drawn to the dry hot climate of the area. Retirement communities are springing up, mobile home parks stretch for miles into the desert surrounding Phoenix and Tucson. Planners in the Phoenix area are desperately trying to find a way of coping with the flood of people from colder regions of the United States, and problems of growth are becoming evident here too, as smog begins to replace the crystal clarity of the desert air. While civic officials try desperately to cope with the flood of people, growth is still officially good in Arizona, and the state is officially dedicated to ever greater importation of water and a rapidly growing population.

The eminent economist Dr. Kenneth Boulding has suggested that Arizona has little to gain by such growth, that the State could perhaps control its rate of growth by abandoning its long-standing efforts to bring more water to its populous central region. He is supported in this by economist Robert Theobald, a resident of Arizona, who suggests that the state may be one of the few in the U.S. that can still choose the sort of future it will have.

A new and different view of water is becoming prevalent among the growing number of Americans who actively oppose the importation of water into the United States from Canada, or from other regions in their own country. Daniel Luten, a geographer at the University of California in Berkeley, suggests that policies which may have been reasonable in an empty land being settled for the first time by industrial man, are questionable and possibly dangerous in a fully developed and populated land. John Kenneth Galbraith is a leader of the growing school of economists who suggest that what was appropiate in a poor society may no longer be so in an affluent society. Priorities change; and now that most people have all the necessities and many luxuries, it is becoming evident that the really scarce commodities are increasingly amenities that were at one time assumed to be free and available to everyone—fresh air, pure water, privacy, silence, green open spaces. Importation of more water is increasingly seen as a threat to these values.

Priorities therefore are changing, and in the face of those changes, many Americans consider it untenable that the same principles of water development that have existed in North America for generations should continue.

Lawrence C. N. Burgess of the Department of Environment in Ottawa, states: "Water problems are, in large part, the creation of an outdated way of thinking... The importance of its uniqueness has been exaggerated out of proportion, especially in the more recent periods in the history of water resource development in North America."

The enormous political and institutional weight behind the traditional ways of thinking are meeting these new attitudes head on, and within the United States itself battle lines are hardening over the water issue. Those Americans who insist that importation into their country of Canadian water will be harmful for ecological, economic, and social reasons, are becoming heard more clearly every day. These may be more effective in the final resolving of the issue than the Canadian attitude.

There are Americans, and Canadians too, who view the question as a moral issue. Convinced that a water shortage does indeed exist in the United States, such people feel that it is the function of a good neighbour to share its life-giving water. David Brower is a leading American conservationist. He answers such arguments this way: "It seems to me that if Canada follows the argument that to be a good neighbour it must give up its wild streams and its wilderness, it can only make that kind of a gift for a short time, then it will have used up its wilderness, its wild streams, and the neighbour to the south will still be thirsty. The neighbour to the south will have grown bigger and bigger and thirstier and thirstier and there will be nowhere else for it to go. I would say that the obligation on the part of the United States right now is to find other solutions, find out how to get along with the part of the world it's already disrupted in the United States and let the wild places on earth, whether in Alaska or Canada or elsewhere, remain that way. Chopping them up, exploiting them, to follow our old habits of growth, would not take long. We could get right through those in a hurry, maybe ten or twenty or thirty years and then what would we have? A world without wilderness. I think we can make the adjustment now, rather than then, to the lasting benefit of all generations we hope to have come."

Along similar lines, American hydrologist and engineer Luna B. Leopold suggests: "I think one could argue that from a moral or ethical standpoint it is an even higher objective to preserve the balance of the landscape, rather than a moral obligation to give your excess water to your neighbour."

A full examination reveals that there is no shortage of water in the United States endangering life or the economy. There are local individual problems, mostly related to pollution and to the unwise use and waste of water. That the United States desperately needs Canadian water is a myth, and in fact, importation of water would in many cases contribute to excessive growth of urban areas, higher costs to those agricultural areas receiving the water, and a loss of markets in other farming areas where similar products are grown. Importation of Canadian water would divert huge quantities of American money from those measures which might assist in the solution of some of the real problems facing the United States.

But in spite of all this, great and growing pressure on Canada can be expected for the diversion of water south to the United States. In the next chapter, the sources of these pressures will be traced.

Chapter 2

Water exports: the growing pressures

Where it can be seen from the lip of the Grand Canyon, the Colorado River far below seems far too small a stream to have created one of the most magnificent spectacles on earth. At closer view the Colorado is a great river, red with the silt it carries as it continues its age-old work of carving the rock of the Arizona and Utah deserts. It can't do so with the same spirit as it once did, however, for the Colorado is now the most dammed, tamed, used and diverted river in the United States. The river's greatest task lies before it, however, because the Colorado is required by United States law to deliver more water than flows between its banks. Meeting that requirement will be even more difficult than carving the Grand Canyon, and the impossibility of it has important implications for Canada. A complex web of water allocations, U.S. water law, Acts of Congress, and power politics is dependent upon the availability of Canadian water, or the promise that it will be available in the future.

The Colorado River has been called the Nile of the Southwest. It begins its 1400 mile journey high in the mountains of Colorado, but for several years none of its water has reached the river's mouth in the Gulf of California in Mexico. It is completely used up during its journey to the sea, yet facilities for use of still more of the River's water have been approved. Development in the states of the upper Colorado will require still more water in the years ahead.

The Colorado story has been one of bitter fighting over its water in the law courts and legislatures of the U.S. In one comic opera case, physical confrontation occurred when the governor of Arizona ordered out troops to prevent California from building a dam across the river. To understand the intricacies of these battles over the Colorado and their implications for Canada, some arithmetic is necessary — it might be called political arithmetic, since the numbers won't add up to the required total.

American law divides the water of the Colorado amongst 3 areas. The upper basin states of Wyoming, Colorado, Utah and New Mexico are allocated 7.5 million acre feet. 7.5 million acre feet are for the use of the region in the southern part of the basin below Lees Ferry, Arizona — the states of Arizona, Nevada and California. By a treaty signed with Mexico in 1944, that country is guaranteed 1.5 million acre feet. This adds up to total commitments of 16.5 million acre feet per year. But the catch is that the river's average flow is only from 13 to 15 million acre feet per year. Unfortunately, 13 million is probably the most realistic figure, since it is based on the average flow since 1930. Even less water than this is expected to flow in the river in the years ahead, for reasons we'll turn to later. Many water experts think an average flow of 11 to 12 million acre feet would be more realistic in planning for the future.

California is presently using about 5.1 million acre feet of the river's water, and this supplies about 80 per cent of the water used by the 10 million people and the rich agriculture of the area. Farming gets most of the water: 4 million acre feet goes to the irrigation districts of southern California, and 1.1 million acre feet is carried 240 miles across the burning heat of the Mojave desert to supply 118 cities, including Los Angeles and San Diego.

The Colorado aqueduct was one of the wonders of the world at the time of its construction in the 1930's; even today the concrete river is an awesome accomplishment with its complex of pumps lifting a billion gallons a day up mountain slopes, and through 92 miles of tunnels. In any environment such an accomplishment would be remarkable; in the heat and desolation of the desert it is phenomenal. But as a result of a United States Supreme Court decision, this aqueduct will likely be only half full in future. This of course is a matter of grave concern in the heavily populated areas of southern California.

The court decision in the case of Arizona vs. California in 1963 culminated 40 years of bitter disputes and 10 years of courtroom battling. It guaranteed to Arizona 2.8 million acre feet of the Colorado's water. Since Nevada is assured .3 million acre feet, that left 4.4 million acre feet for southern California, and as we have noted, the state is already using 5.1 million acre feet.

In keeping with the arguments of such economists as James Crutchfield or William Martin, the obvious solution to the problem would be to divert .7 million acre feet from low valued agricultural crops such as hay and grain to the cities, which can afford to pay much higher prices for it. But there is another catch in the complexities of American water law. More than half of the water destined for urban use in the Colorado aqueduct is "junior" to the claims of the irrigation districts on the river. The cities, already paying more than $25 per acre foot wholesale water, cannot buy water being used for irrigation since it is reserved by law for agriculture at prices as low as about $2 per acre foot.

Arizona isn't using its full allotment of the river's water yet, but for many years it has been promoting a project that would bring water into the central region of the state, the Phoenix-Tucson area. Here it would be used to offset in part the "overdraft" currently being pumped from the aquifer under the Sonoran Desert. The scheme is called the Central Arizona Project. Pumping stations will lift water 1200 feet out of the Lake Havasu reservoir on the Colorado River. At a cost of $1.2 billion dollars, the CAP would bring 1.2 million acre feet to central Arizona.

The Central Arizona Project was approved by Congress in 1968, following a great deal of interstate in-fighting, legal manoeuvering, and pressure politics. Relatively small amounts of money have so far been approved for the project, however; just enough to provide for the technical planning process. But when water starts moving through the CAP canal, the strange arithmetic of the river will begin to cause serious problems. The only slack that would save the system from shortages of water is to be found in the upper Colorado as long as those states are not making full use of their allotments. Such a respite would be only temporary.

Even at that, the problems are just beginning. Strangely, efforts to make the greatest possible use of the Colorado River have resulted in there being less water in the river. And what remains has suffered a sharp drop in quality. When great dams stop the flow of the water and spread it out in huge reservoirs in the desert, a lot of it is evaporated by the hot dry climate. Lake Mead is the reservoir behind the Hoover Dam (formerly Boulder Dam). It loses a million acre feet a year to the desert air, a vertical depth of 7 feet of water, evaporated from that great impoundment with its 550 mile shoreline. Add to that losses from the two reservoirs downstream behind the Parker and Davis Dams, and more than a million and a half acre feet must be written off each year — enough to supply a population of 4 million people. Additionally, Lake Powell, behind the Glen Canyon Dam upstream from Hoover, is still being filled though its gates were closed in 1963. Up to 25 per cent of the water seeps out through the porous rock of the reservoir sides, adding to losses from evaporation.

But not only is a lot of water lost; what remains is of sharply reduced quality, containing ever more concentrated quantities of salts. The Colorado in its natural state is quite salty. Before Hoover Dam was built to even out the great variations in the flow of the river, there were 200 parts per million of salt in it. Now it is 700 parts per million at Hoover Dam, 800 at Parker Dam, and 900 parts per million at the dam which diverts water into the Imperial Valley, one of the world's greatest irrigation projects.

Salt concentration in the Colorado River continues to rise by 10 million parts per year, and it poses a threat to the life of the valley. "I think the problems of salt in the Imperial Valley are very, very serious," says California's Director of Water Resources, William Gianelli. "Ultimately, I think the Imperial Valley is going to have to receive a better quality water than it is receiving, and I think that if that is not done, the future of the Imperial Valley is not bright. I think it could be disastrous for many parts of that area."

As the Colorado cut and shaped the Grand Canyon, the silt it wore from the rock was carried far downstream. Much of that soil was deposited in what is now the Imperial Valley, where it lies a mile deep under the lush green of the prosperous looking farms. The soil has always been salty, and several acre feet of water must be sluiced through it to wash away that salt before crops can be grown. This is a continuing process, and as the irrigation water becomes more salty, still more of it is required to keep washing the salt from the root level of the soil. Officials of the Imperial Irrigation District consider the addition of new, salt-free water to the Colorado essential if farming is to remain possible in the future. There is of course no way that agriculture can pay for the water required, since augmenting the Colorado will certainly cost more than $50 per acre foot, and farms in the valley currently pay just over $2 per acre foot. However, the people of the district see Mexico as their ace in the hole.

Mexico has long been guaranteed 1.5 million acre feet of water in the Colorado River. But the Mexicans are at the end of the line, and by the time they receive the water, it has greatly deteriorated through evaporation, and through use and re-use in the irrigated fields of the United States. The River carries more than a thousand parts per million when it enters Mexico, a disastrous level for Mexican farmers. Many of their fields have been forced out of production as the salt accumulates in the soil.

The Colorado River Basin Project Act of 1968 transferred to the U.S. federal government responsibility for seeing that Mexico gets its 1.5 million acre feet of water, a commitment for which the Colorado River states had been responsible up to that time. But quantity, understandably, wasn't enough for Mexico, and that country threatened to sue the U.S. in the World Court unless the water was of sufficiently high quality to be useful. Carl Bevins, president of the Imperial Irrigation District, is convinced that the federal government will have to meet this international requirement for better water in the Colorado by augmenting the river's flow far upstream with new, clean water.

The farm corporations of the Imperial Valley see themselves riding on the coat-tails of U.S. agreements with Mexico, because better water for that country, paid for by the federal government to meet an international commitment, will be going right by their diversion facilities. They could get more water, and better water, at little cost to themselves. The source of that new water must ultimately be Canada according to many California water authorities.

With such problems already facing the states along the Colorado River, it is amazing to find that further uses of its water are being approved or planned. In the "Four Corners" area where Arizona, Colorado, New Mexico and Utah meet, a complex of six enormous coal-fired electric power plants are planned. One already is in operation, pouring into the clear desert air more particulate matter than all the polluters of New York and Los Angeles combined. The six plants will, when built, provide a cover of smog for many of the most beautiful American national parks and monuments, including the Grand Canyon. They will consume more than a hundred and fifty thousand tons of coal a day, much of it stripped from the ancestral lands of the Navajo and Hopi Indians.

Power plants require enormous quantities of water for cooling purposes. The six-plant complex will require up to 370 thousand acre feet of water per year, much of it being supplied from the Colorado River. Evaporation of the water warmed by the power plants and returned to the Colorado River will increase the salinity of the Colorado by about five per cent. With its salt content already a major problem, this will provide further impetus to the drive to improve the quality of the water of the Colorado by mixing into it large quantities of fresh water from elsewhere.

The almost desperate search for more energy will likely in future have an even greater effect on the river. The oil shales of Colorado, Wyoming and Utah have long been considered a possible source of oil to supplement the conventional oil resources of North America as they become depleted. In 1971 the United States government initiated new studies of methods that might make the process economical. Hydrogenation or "gasifying" coal from the large deposits of the western United States is also considered a possible source of supply of fossil fuel. In both cases, huge quantities of water would be required. This is the watershed of the Colorado River; it would be Colorado River water that would be used and the portion of it that returned to the river after use would inevitably be of poorer quality than before.

These new and projected large-scale industrial uses of the water of the Colorado River, added to expected population growth and the already serious problems existing on the river, brings the water problem to crisis proportions in the minds of a great many citizens of the American Southwest. For instance, Rich Johnson, executive director of the Central Arizona Project Association, says: "The Central Arizona Project is only going to bring in a million acre feet to the Phoenix-Tucson area, which won't offset the loss of ground water by pumping. So obviously we have to look beyond the Central Arizona Project for another source of water, we just have to. This Central Arizona Project is a beginning in the right direction, but we can't stop there by any means, because if we do, within a very few years we'll be right back where we were before."

Throughout the American Southwest, service club luncheons and chambers of commerce are frequently treated to discussions of the issues involved in a manner much like a speech delivered to the American Bar Association by California's Attorney General. "I would like to state now, as frankly as I can, what I foresee for the future to handle that combination of a population explosion and the continuing migration to the Southwest: I foresee huge regional water projects. I envision great man-made rivers of surplus water flowing from water-rich areas, such as the Pacific

Northwest, to water deficient areas, such as the Colorado River Basin."

Since 1963, when the decades-long battle between California and Arizona over the water of the Colorado was ended by a court decision, these states have been united in driving toward eventual augmentation of the Colorado. The Colorado River Basin Project Act of 1968, the act which approved the Central Arizona Project, brought the other five states along the Colorado into line with this long term goal. Agreement on the Central Arizona project was only possible when the governors of all the Colorado Basin states agreed that more water must flow into the Colorado, and then they became politically co-ordinated to achieve this goal. Traditionally fighting among themselves over who would get how much of the Colorado River, only a cause that would ensure each state all the water it wanted could bring them together.

There was no doubt in anyone's mind that the source of that water would be the Columbia River, the great stream rising in British Columbia and flowing through the states of Washington and Oregon. It pours into the Pacific Ocean ten times as much water as flows in the Colorado — more than one hundred and thirty million acre feet each year. Secretary of the Interior Stewart Udall in 1965 said: "We don't think it even wise to study anything other than that source, meaning from the Columbia River below Bonneville Dam. . ." The concept most commonly projected suggests a canal 900 miles long carrying 8 or 9 million acre feet annually from The Dalles on the Columbia to Lake Mead, the reservoir behind Hoover Dam on the Colorado near Las Vegas. The cost would total several billion dollars.

Washington and Oregon of course opposed any legal options on their water, and Washington's powerful Senator Henry M. Jackson, Chairman of the U.S. Senate Interior and Insular Affairs Committee, forced acceptance of a provision in the 1968 Act that forbids the U.S. Government even to study any sort of diversion into the Colorado from any river basin outside of the seven Colorado River states. Since those states were all totally committed to the principle that water had to be imported from outside basins, it was a tough provision to swallow. But they did, since it was the price of getting an act of any kind passed, and it was the only way in which the Central Arizona Project could be assured of federal funding.

The states of the Colorado had powerful support from the

water development agencies. The Bureau of Reclamation, one of the two great dambuilding agencies in the United States, had for many years been studying various ways of moving water from the Columbia to the Colorado. Along with its supporting lobbies, it was therefore actively supporting a project which would have kept it busy and well funded for many years. Senator Jackson, in rejecting any suggestion that the Bureau be charged with the task of officially studying the feasibility of such a diversion, said: "To ask any agency whose business is to construct water projects whether it is necessary to divert the Columbia is something like asking an automobile salesman's advice on whether you should purchase a new car."

So the battle lines were drawn. Factors favouring diversion of the Columbia southward included support of the seven Colorado River states with their great Congressional power, the politically potent dam building agencies, and a public which had been convinced of the desperate need of the Southwest, even though their per capita use of water was among the highest and their water costs among the lowest in the U.S. Facing these forces, the states of the Pacific Northwest could find little comfort in the ten-year moratorium on water diversion studies provided for in the 1968 Act. The position of American states differs from that of Canadian provinces in that the states cannot veto water diversion projects approved by the federal government, as the provinces of Canada appear able to do. The Northwest states would have no veto if the much greater population and political power of the Colorado states were at some future time to get their way in Congress. And so Washington and Oregon, Idaho and Montana, looked for ways to hedge their bets.

The Colorado River Basin Project Act of 1968 includes in it provision for protection of the area in which the water originates. That is, if the Pacific Northwest states were at some future time to need for their own use the water that might be diverted to the Southwest out of the Columbia, it would have prior right to that water. If that water could best be replaced by importing it from elsewhere, the state would be guaranteed against having to pay more for that water than it would have cost to use its own water, had it not been diverted.

Of course, once water from the Columbia was diverted into the Colorado and put to full use, no one would expect the flow to be cut off. So to fulfill this part of the act, two alternatives are possible. Those states receiving the water could make payment to the areas of origin for giving up their prior rights to the water. Or, a deal could be made whereby the water diverted south would be replaced from another source when required. That source could only be Canada.

The first alternative, that of paying a state for giving up its rights to water diverted out of it, amounts in fact to payment for the water. This is a principle that the drier areas of the United States have always refused to consider in any way. In the U.S., water law has been rooted in the idea that those who make use of the water first, have a right to it. Payment for water diverted from another region would have ramifications for a vast number of existing and planned water development projects in the U.S. This issue has been fought out in California, where the water users of the south have refused to pay for the water diverted from the North by the State Water Project. Joseph Jenson, Chairman of the powerful Metropolitan Water District of Southern California, insists that there is no way that the Colorado River states would pay for water from Canada — rather, it would help pay for the facilities for moving it. Suggestions that water be paid for within the United States are even less tenable.

And so, to the hard-pressed states of the Pacific Northwest, the logical thing is to try to assure that water diverted from their river will be guaranteed replacement by Canada if at any time in the future it were needed. Governor Tom McCall of Oregon has pressed for immediate negotiations with Canada. "I think we ought to start yesterday, yesterday's not soon enough. Go to the President of the United States and the Secretary of State, and work with your Prime Minister and your Secretary of State on the problem of under what terms you would spare water to us and how much it would cost. I mean, we're not going to try to pull any power play on you, try to steal it from you, extort it from you. But what is a reasonable basis, so you would be remunerated sufficiently, and it would still be economical for us to do it?" Such an agreement, Governor McCall feels, would be essential before any water could move from the Columbia to the Colorado.

This position has been adopted by the governors of all the western states. Meeting in Seattle in 1969, they directed attention away from the question of transferring water from the American Pacific Northwest to the Southwest, to a promotion of immediate negotiation with Canada. It wasn't affection for one another that brought the states together. It seems much more likely that fear, fear in the Northwest of the enormous political power of the Southwest, was the glue that made the bond. In a moment of candour, Governor Tom McCall of Oregon talked about the problems involved in sharing the Columbia River with his drier neighbours: "We'd have to look at it very carefully, because they are so much more powerful than we are, and this gentle, benign camel will get his nose under our tent, you see. And with their having twenty times the Congressional strength that we have for example we'd have to be very chary about moving even an inch in that direction... there would be a tremendous danger once they get the taste of that water, that we'd ever get any sort of concessions back from them or any sort of sympathy, either."

The McCall administration conducted a detailed study of future needs for water in the state of Oregon, and to no one's surprise it indicated the state would be short of water in future. It said: "Oregon will be a water deficient state, in the year 2070, because it does not have enough water originating within its borders to fulfill its total requirement. The annual undepleted flow of all the basins in Oregon, equalled or exceeded in 4 of 5 years, was found to be 65,940,000 acre-feet, and the total demand has been projected to be 80,380,000 acre feet in the year 2070."

Oregon has been urging the other states of the Pacific Northwest to rush their studies of future water needs to completion, anticipating of course that their findings will be similar to those of Oregon. "The region will need cold, hard facts—not emotional arguments, to resist the Southwest's thirst for our water." Preliminary estimates from Washington, Idaho and Montana indicate that they too expect to be short of water within a century.

The Oregon study is a fascinating document. It appears to provide for water for a densely populated, highly industrialized state with irrigated agriculture on every acre of land to which water could be piped. It is a future that Oregon, of all states in the U.S., is trying to avoid. The McCall administration is doing what it can to slow the growth of the state, to preserve its present amenities. It has the example of California immediately to its south to show the effect of unlimited growth, and Oregonians want no part of a similar sort of development in their state. Their water study, however, presumes that this sort of growth will in fact take place.

In developing these figures of enormous requirements that support its claim of shortages in future, Oregon has made some interesting assumptions. One reads: "Economic justification and feasibility will be kept in the background and will not limit or restrict the various uses of water." Another is: "A knowledge of the supply of water available within a basin will not influence the estimate of the water requirements for each of the beneficial uses."

Such assumptions are of course completely out of step with modern thinking in water resources. It seems altogether likely that Governor Tom McCall and his administration are very much aware of this — but the fact in which they must take comfort is that these assumptions cannot be questioned by the southwestern states as they look thirstily at the water of the Columbia, because these are precisely the assumptions and principles upon which the Southwest bases *its* claim of water shortages. One suspects that Governor McCall gets wry satisfaction from this situation.

It is clear, then, that ancient principles of water use which are plainly outdated and show every sign of declining into disrepute in the United States itself, are the basis on which the western American states have joined in demanding their government negotiate for Canadian water. The political reasons for these states clinging to this sort of reasoning are clear, and rooted in decades of history. Canada need labour under no such handicaps in considering the inevitable requests for water from south of the border.

The greatest pressure for water export is likely to materialize as a result of this course of events already underway in the Colorado and Columbia states. But the call for Canadian water will not be limited to these regions. In fact, many observers have predicted that if export of Canadian water occurs, it will begin with the Great Lakes. Some of the reasons for this are to be found far to the south.

In the lush irrigated cotton fields of the high plains of west Texas, the wells go deeper each year as the farm corporations use the ground water in unlimited quantities. After 1980, there is every indication that the irrigation boom which got underway in the 1940's will begin to collapse as the water is exhausted. It was in a desperate effort to find a way of preventing this at little cost to the area itself that the Texas Water Plan was unveiled in 1968.

The plan would bring 12 or 13 million acre feet of water from the Mississippi river 600 miles across Arkansas and Oklahoma, or across Louisiana if a more southerly route is chosen. It would have to be pumped uphill more than 3000 feet, a process that would require seven million kilowatts of electricity, or about 40 per cent of all the power presently generated in the state. Reservoirs of the Texas Water Plan would flood some two million acres of fine valley bottomland, and would essentially eliminate all the wild rivers of east Texas. The whole thing is estimated to cost thirteen and a half billion dollars, and water delivered to the high plains would cost, at $168 per acre foot, about ten times what the farmers growing the already subsidized crops could afford to pay for it. Obviously, someone else will be paying the shot.

The reaction to all this on the part of the people of Louisiana, downstream from where the water would be removed, can be imagined. The bayous of that state owe their existence to the flow of the river, and the estuaries that nurture the life of the Gulf of Mexico depend on the flow of fresh water that mingles with the salt water along the coast. Senator Russell Long of Louisiana has said: "Texas will get our water over my dead body." Other political figures and newspapers in the state have echoed that sentiment. Opposition is growing upstream, too.

In 1969, voters in Texas turned down a 3.5 billion dollar bond issue designed to get work started on the project as a lever to get the much larger federal funds required to see it through. In true Texas style, it was the largest bond issue ever floated anywhere in the world. In spite of its defeat, work on various aspects of the Plan proceeds on a piecemeal basis. John Connally, who heartily approved of the Texas Water Plan when he was governor of the state, served for a time in Washington as Secretary of the Treasury — the source from which most of the money for the project must come. He continues to be influential in the Nixon administration.

Now, where does Canada fit into all of this? Suppose that the 13 million acre feet the Texas plan requires could be replaced, thereby assuring Louisiana that its interests would not be affected. The fighting edge of its opposition certainly would be dulled. As Professor George Whetstone of Texas Tech University has put it: "The potentiality of augmenting the Mississippi by importation of Canadian water could avoid an impasse."

To accomplish this, William Ackerman of the Illinois State Water Survey has suggested that water from the Great Lakes could be diverted south by expanding an existing diversion out of Lake Michigan at Chicago; a diversion which currently flushes that city's sewage down the Illinois River to the Mississippi. Other diversions out of Lake Michigan would provide for growth around its shores. Ackerman, and other water planners too, have suggested diversion of Great Lakes water southward into the Ohio River. This would provide water for urban centres south of Lake Erie from Detroit to Buffalo, and would flush their sewage south to the Ohio instead of north into Lake Erie, as occurs at present. It is the old idea of moving pollution somewhere else instead of getting on with the business of stopping it. As U.S. economist Dr. James Crutchfield has said: "Dilution has proved to be basically unsatisfactory as a technique for dealing with long-run problems of water quality."

The Ohio is of course a major tributary of the Mississippi. Such plans would add water to the total volume of the Mississippi and presumably it would be available for withdrawal by Texas or New Mexico or for whatever "Grand Plan" evolved downstream. But even the most fanatical proponent of big ditches might be expected to pause before spreading across country the water of a Mississippi loaded with the wastes of the industrial heart of America. The mingling of this sadly overburdened water with that of cleaner streams and pure underground water could have drastic consequences.

The level of the Great Lakes would be maintained through all of this manipulation by diverting south rivers in Ontario and Quebec that presently flow northward into James Bay and Hudson Bay. Another proposal for increasing the flow of the Mississippi would involve diverting Canadian water into it from the Prairie provinces via the Milk or Souris Rivers — possibilities which fit neatly into present water development proposals for that part of Canada.

The water system of New York City is notable for waste, pollution, administrative chaos and political opportunism. As noted in the previous chapter, it would be difficult to make a case for the importation of water from Canada or anywhere to solve the water problems of the region, but the U.S. Army Corps of engineers is laying the groundwork for just such an effort. A study authorized by Congress in 1965 and completed in 1969 envisions an almost complete engineering of the waterways of the Atlantic Northeast to provide for continued growth in the New York area—and some aspects of the plan reach up to Canada.

The study, called "Feasibility Report on Alternative Regional Water Supply Plans for Northern New Jersey-New York City-Western Connecticut Metropolitan Area," envisions sequential development that would result in "ultimately a diversion from Lake Ontario to the Mohawk River." Presumably, here again southward diversions of Canadian rivers would be required to maintain lake levels.

The Great Lakes-St. Lawrence system would be affected again further downstream. The report suggests diversion south to New York of water from Lake Champlain. The Lake now drains north in the Richelieu River through beautiful Quebec farmland to join the St. Lawrence at Sorel. Canadians would have company in their concern about such a manipulation, since Lake Champlain forms almost half the border between Vermont and New York state. One Vermont official angrily stated that, "they can start a war if they try this. Lake Champlain is sacred to Vermonters."

Both American and Canadian spokesmen insist that no formal consideration has been given to the possibility of export of Canadian water to the United States. This is undoubtedly true. But it is clear that many water development plans proposed or proceeding in the U.S. require the eventual importation of Canadian water for their completion. Perhaps even more important than the development of these physical plans is the widespread acceptance of the idea amongst Americans that in the natural course of events Canadian water must eventually flow south.

The absorption of this idea into the American consciousness has occurred in a number of ways. Its main thrust began on a grand scale when in 1964 the Ralph Parsons Engineering Company of Los Angeles launched its "NAWAPA" plan. (North American Water and Power Alliance). This idea of a continent-wide plan that would move perhaps 100 million acre feet of mainly Canadian water into the United States each year quickly caught the support of many dry-state politicians. One of the most enthusiastic was Senator Frank Moss of Utah. His interest can perhaps be explained by a line from his book, *The Water Crisis*. He says: "Increasingly, the control of water becomes the key to prosperity, growth, and political and economic power in the United States." It's a sentiment Canadians should recognize and ponder.

Through the remainder of the sixties, a torrent of continental water development plans were spawned, and the subject was discussed at numberless scientific and engineering conferences. With the popularization of the idea, funds for research into various aspects of large-scale water diversion became available to water research centres established at universities throughout the United States. That most prestigious of academic gatherings, the annual meeting of the American Association for the Advancement of Science, convened a special symposium in December 1968 on the subject of water importation into arid lands. A common pattern at this and similar gatherings has been a recognition of all sorts of scientific imponderables and potential disasters that might follow large scale water diversions, usually concluded by statements such as that of Professor Gerald W. Thomas at the 1968 AAAS meeting. He said: "Movement of vast amounts of water from areas of 'surplus' to areas of deficiency appears to be inevitable." Professor Arthur Pillsbury of the University of California in Los Angeles is more specific, stating: "The only real source is from Canada."

Politicians, many academics, water development agencies and their supporting lobbies, have insisted that water importation is essential in areas facing almost any sort of water supply problem. As Governor Jack Williams of Arizona puts it: "We're an oasis and consequently we must continually seek new sources of water in order to keep up with the modern progress that requires more showers, more dishwashers, more of everything." It's really not surprising that in such areas as the dry Southwest of the United States, or the Texas high plains, or the cities of the Northeast during drought periods, the "need" for massive water imports has become a self-evident truth for perhaps the majority of the citizens.

There are of course many alternative approaches to the problems of these areas apart from massive water importation. The more efficient use of existing water supplies, the allocation of water to higher value uses, the pricing of water at reasonable levels — these and many other obvious steps in approaching a problem of water shortages have so far received little more than lip service. Such moves would require the reappraisal of political legal traditions of considerable historic standing. Though irrelevant to the needs of today, these institutional complications are such that the "easy way out" is simply to bring in more water from other regions. It's cheap, too, since water projects benefitting a particular area are normally paid for by taxpayers of the entire state or nation. If Canadian water becomes involved, the people of Canada will pay too, either directly or indirectly. That is the lesson of the Columbia River Treaty, as we will see later.

In the previous chapter it was shown how water importation would be for the maintenance and increase of irrigated agriculture, except in the case of the New York projects. A few simple facts show how this will result in pressure for Canadian water. First, the desert and semi-arid lands of the Southwest are of almost no value for any purpose without water. Second, the adding of water to dry land can overnight increase its value from almost nothing to $1,000 or more per acre. Third, agriculture in these dry regions is carried on by a small number of large farm corporations, and the family farm is almost non-existent. Fourth, the land is largely owned by very big corporations — oil companies, land holding companies, banks. The prospect of receiving subsidized water to grow crops at guaranteed subsidized prices on land that water has caused to appreciate enormously in value is, to say the least, attractive. The large land holding companies, oil companies, banks and conglomerates that own the land wield the sort of power that can make such dreams come true.

There are additional members of the "water establishment". There are the contractors who would build the enormous structures required for water movement, concrete and other materials companies, construction equipment firms, water development and distribution agencies and their supporting lobbies. Clearly, the most powerful elements of the political, social and economic structures stand to gain most from water importation. The pressures on politicians that all of these groups can generate are enormous. As the authoritative text *Water Supply* puts it: "When the benefits go to a well-defined interest group for whom it is worthwhile making the political investments necessary to assure passage of the legislature, while the costs are dispersed so widely as not to justify anyone's organizing political opposition, special interest groups are all too likely to win out against the general public."

For the all too human politician, the grand structure with

a bronze plaque bearing his name is a prospect that has to receive secret contemplation, since it is a common reward for those who make smooth the path of water development legislation. As *Water Supply* says: "The gravy train runs in the same direction as the glory trail."

Some of the greatest concentrations of political power in the U.S. are to be found in the regions that have experienced water shortages, as in the northeastern states; or that are naturally dry, such as Texas and the Southwest; or that might be attracted by an easy though illusory way out of the pollution problems through dilution of wastes by new, clean water from Canada, as in the industrial regions of the North. There exists therefore a powerful group in the United States Congress favouring importation of water from Canada. As noted earlier, the governors of the western states have agreed that Canada holds the answer to their water problems. The Secretary of the Interior in the Nixon administration, Rogers Morton, stated that his country will have to consider plans to import water from the Arctic through Canada. His predecessor in office, Walter Hickel, on the subject of water relationships between Canada and the U.S., said: "Look down the road 10 years from now . . . and it's entirely possible we'll have to have a whole network tying together the rivers of the west." President Richard Nixon in February 1970 instructed the State Department to work out a continental energy deal with Canada—and though water was not explicitly included, many in both countries feel it would logically follow any agreement on oil, gas, and electricity. As David Cass-Beggs, Chairman of Manitoba Hydro, has pointed out, energy and water are indivisible.

So although no formal request for Canadian water has yet been made, the plans, the politics, the institutions, the vested interests, the public attitudes, all point to growing pressure for Canadian water from south of the border in the years ahead. As was shown in the previous chapter, no genuine need for Canadian water exists in the United States, and expressions of need are the result of complex historical and political processes that we have tried to outline here. There is clearly no moral question of granting or denying water to a thirsty neighbour. The only possible justification for water export would therefore be if great economic, social and other benefits would accrue to Canada, and if environmental and political costs involved would be minimal. These questions will now be explored in detail.

Chapter 3
Water exports: the Canadian response

When former minister of Energy, Mines and Resources, Joe Greene, was asked to outline the position of the Canadian Government regarding the export to the United States of Canadian water, he stated: "It's the same as it is in regard to any of our other energy resources, namely that if there is an amount that is clearly surplus to Canadian need, present or future, then that energy source is for sale to the extent of that surplus. With regard to water, we do not know whether there is a surplus because we do not have sufficient inventory of our total waters. We do not know what is the Canadian need for the future . . . We don't know that there is a surplus and therefore there is none for sale. That is the Canadian position."

This is about the way that provincial governments have expressed their attitude to the question of water export too. The minister responsible until recently for British Columbia's water resources, Ray Williston, has put it this way. "We do not know how much water we need and where we will ultimately need it, not only in British Columbia but in other parts of Canada. Therefore, at this time, our answer to any water diversion policy has had to be 'No'." Five years earlier, Premier W.A.C. Bennett had said: "Even to talk about selling water is ridiculous. Water is our heritage and you don't sell your heritage." Similar expressions of policy have been made by present and former governments in Alberta.

So the official stand of Canada's governments seems clear. But how firm is that position?

In an election campaign speech in 1965, Prime Minister Lester Pearson stated that Canada had plenty of water, and went on: "The United States is finding that water is one of its most valuable and is becoming one of its scarcest resources . . . The question of water resources . . . is a continental and international problem. We have to be careful not to alienate this resource without taking care of our own needs and we will be discussing this with the United States who are very anxious to work out arrangements by which some of our water resources are moved down south. This can be as important as exporting wheat or oil."

But Minister of Northern Affairs Arthur Laing reversed the government's ground just a few days later, saying: "Diversion of Canadian water to the U. S. is not negotiable. There is no such thing as a continental resource. We own it." That seems firm enough. Yet Walter Stewart, writing in *Maclean's*, March, 1970, recalls a discussion with Mr. Laing at about the time of his forthright declaration. "After I had put away my notebook and was about to leave his office, he said, 'You should know, for your own information, that something like NAWAPA (the huge 100 million acre feet water export plan) is not merely feasible, it's inevitable.' When I asked him why, then, we seemed to be repudiating it, he bobbed his head sagely and said, 'We are establishing a bargaining position, and the best bargaining position is to say "NO" '."

Mr. Pearson's successor, Prime Minister Pierre Trudeau, was accused in a 1970 television program of being prepared to export Canadian water. In his answer Mr. Trudeau referred to resources generally, including water. "I don't want to be a dog in the manger about this. But if people are not going to use it, can't we sell it for good hard cash?" His Northern Affairs Minister, Jean Chrétien (Mr. Laing's successor), seemed to be harbouring similar sentiments when he said, according to *Time* magazine of May 2, 1969: "Within 25 years we will be exporting water."

Tracing the position of Minister of the Environment Jack Davis is intriguing, particularly since his department is now responsible for water resources, and since the environmental ramifications of water diversions are enormous. Back in 1964, Mr. Davis was quoted in the Vancouver *Sun:* "The plans of MP Jack Davis for the diversion of northern water to central Canada and the United States are passing the state of imaginative conception to that of practical consideration. Mr. Davis' address Monday to the Pacific Northwest Trade Association in Prince George devoted more attention to the necessary mechanics of this gigantic scheme than to its attractive benefits. 'To pour the waters of the Yukon, the MacKenzie, the Athabasca, the Nelson, and the Hurricanaw into thirsty southern Canada and the Central United States is an inspiring conception' ."

Two years later, at a Columbia River Water Congress in Wenatchee, Washington, Davis was even more enthusiastic.

"I want you to think of schemes which are not only basin wide but possibly even continental in scope. The Rocky Mountains need no longer contain our thoughts. We can vault over them or tunnel through them and see what lies beyond . . . so we will be turning whole rivers around." Political reality forced him to point out that actual export was probably some time off, but years later, on June 6, 1970, in Edmonton, at a Liberal policy convention, Mr. Davis said Canada might be missing a bet in not selling water to the United States. He was critical of party members who called for caution in the sale of natural resources, suggesting that the U. S. might develop a commercial method for extracting fresh water from salt water, and that Canada would then have lost a lot of money by not selling fresh water to the U.S. in the meantime.

Many people have travelled an environmental "Road to Damascus" in recent years, and it seems that with respect to water, Mr. Davis trod that path in the summer of 1970. For by October, just 4 months after his Edmonton declaration he had switched so far in his thinking, or perhaps just in his perception of political realities, that he outlined to a Burnaby, B.C., Liberal gathering his "ironclad rules" for water. They were:

1. Don't export water to the U.S.A. (because you'll never be able to cut off the flow).
2. Don't divert whole rivers from one river basin to the next.
3. Don't regulate water flow in such a way as to jeopardize other renewable resources in the area.
4. Don't sacrifice trees, fish, wildlife and other living things for the production of power or the protection of real estate unless absolutely necessary.

"If we apply these rules," said Mr. Davis, "we will say an emphatic 'No' to the diversion of Canadian waters, in bulk, into the U.S.A."

These "rules" are particularly interesting not only because the "no export" stand is a reversal of the position he advocated four months earlier, but also because the last three rules are being grossly violated in water development all across Canada without visible opposition by the government of Canada. Additionally, Mr. Davis had never declared himself officially on this issue in the House of Commons.

The New Democratic Party takes an unconditional "no export" stand on this question, based on the conviction that there will be no surplus as Canada's economy grows. The Progressive Conservative Party seems to be occupying about the same grounds as the Liberals — no export until we know how much water we have and how much we are going to need. At least, that's the position of party leader Robert Stanfield, but at a Conservative Party policy conference at Niagara Falls in the fall of 1969, delegates recommended that Canada should actively undertake research into methods of exporting surplus water to the United States. Former Conservative resources minister Alvin Hamilton has long advocated water export, and he suggested at the conference that water be included along with other energy resources in negotiations with the United States.

The export of Canadian water to the United States is advocated with varying degrees of enthusiasm by a number of Canadian academics, engineering and construction interests, and government development agencies. There are a number of assumptions that characterize the advocacy of water export, and they bear examination. To accomplish this, it is necessary to examine in some detail proposals and attitudes of a few leading groups and individuals who have involved themselves in this question.

First and probably most important is the assumption that there is a great and growing need for water in the United States, and that the situation will be critical before long. In chapter one it was seen that this simply is not true, and that water importation could in fact aggravate some of the more serious problems in the United States, rather than provide relief for a mythical national thirst. In chapter two we saw where the pressures were coming from that have perpetuated the myth of "The Water Crisis." The effectiveness of these pressures and their accompanying publicity programs have been evident in the almost unquestioned acceptance in Canada that such a "crisis" exists. Many of those people in Canada most opposed to water export, and most horrified by its probable consequences, concede that the need exists or soon will, and that the enormous political and economic power of the United States will at some point force Canada to sell water to the Americans.

The Canadian group most active in perpetuating the myth of the great American thirst has been the Canadian Water Resources Association. It has long promoted water development in Canada, and its spokesmen appear to consider water export a natural outgrowth of this. In 1970, CWRA president Dr. John Hare told the Association's annual meeting that the United States would be short 50 to 100 million gallons of water a year by 1980 if other sources were not found. "At this time the U.S. is in great danger and the Americans are well aware of it," said Dr. Hare. A year later, Dr. Hare was suggesting that the United States would be needing an additional 120 million acre feet of water within the next 20 to 30 years.

Dr. Hare and his organization are of course not alone in accepting uncritically the simple projections of present growth in use of water in the United States as an indication of future need. Recently, however, the fact that these projections of need bear no relationship to the actual state of water requirements in the U.S. has become evident even to some of those in Canada who have long been promoting export of water. Dr. Arleigh Laycock of the University of Alberta, for example, seldom refers to great physical need for water south of the border, but rather suggests that the sale of Canadian water could be a great economic boon to Canada. "If water is worth say 40 dollars per acre-foot, we might conceivably by exporting only one percent of our supply, gain a gross revenue of a billion dollars per year, from the sale of this water. This could be a very important item in our economy — it could be a far greater export than wheat." The Hon. Alvin Hamilton in his advocacy of water export told the 1971 annual convention of the Canadian Water Resources Association that export of 6 or 7 per cent of Canada's water should be worth 360 to 400 billion dollars . . . a flight of fancy that differs from those of other water export promoters only in degree.

At the moment no market exists for Canadian water in the United States, and recognition of this has led some export enthusiasts to take a different approach to the subject. Professor Edward Kuiper of the Univeristy of Manitoba, who devised one large export plan, now considers that costs of export are so great that any discussion of the issue is premature. Dr. Laycock recognises that there is no way the Americans would pay a price for Canadian water that would make it even remotely practical for Canada, although this is small comfort to those who oppose export since economics is seldom allowed to interfere with the politics of water development. Since actual export doesn't seem reasonable at the moment, Dr. Laycock has taken quite a different tack. As a "bridge" to the large export projects, he would like to see Canada sell options on its water for future delivery. That is, for payment today, Canada would guarantee water at a time in the future when the United States might want it. Laycock suggests that the Americans would not have to go to the trouble of straightening out the legal and political chaos of their water systems; that they could continue and increase their excessive demands on underground water supplies; and that they could proceed with interbasin transfers in the United States, knowing that the area of origin of that water would get it replaced from Canada on demand. In other words, a sale of options on Canadian water would encourage the U.S. so to complicate their water situation that they would create a crisis where none now exists, rather than setting about solving their problems. Having collected money through the years, Canadians of that future period when the Americans needed or wanted to exercise their options, would have no opportunity to consider whether or not they wished to export water. Their birthright would have been sold by an earlier generation. The Americans would quite rightly consider that Canada had been paid for rights that were no longer negotiable.

The attractiveness of this sort of idea in the United States was shown by the election of Dr. Laycock to the presidency of the American Water Resources Association in 1971. At meetings all over North America he has proposed "option agreements" and small scale exports that might set a precedent for larger export schemes. These he calls "phased, sequential" development. This is an accurate way of describing the sequence of water development after the first stage is undertaken. Dr. Laycock would suggest that each incremental development would be carried out as a matter of choice when economics seemed to indicate its advisability, but we will see that experience indicates such a progression of developments is an inevitability for quite different reasons—reasons inherent in the nature of rivers and their relationship with the land.

To American audiences, Dr. Laycock has outlined means whereby they might apply pressure to have preliminary yet far-reaching proposals adopted. To Canadian audiences he has stressed the enormous economic benefits he sees in water export, while deriding those who see danger in such schemes to Canada politically and environmentally.

We have noted that Canadian policy states no consideration can be given to the question of water export until detailed studies show clearly how much water Canada has, how much will be needed in the future, and whether there remains an amount surplus to our needs. A characteristic assumption of those who would export Canadian water, and in fact of a great many other Canadians too, is that this nation possesses enormous surpluses of water. This appears to be obvious when adding up the volumes of water carried in the great rivers of the nation. Professor Kuiper of the University of Manitoba has said: "The regions with surplus are in the North and Northwest where at the present time hundreds of millions of acre feet of water per year are discharged into the sea without having been of any use to the Canadian people." Professor Kuiper sees minimal need for this water in the north, and concludes that up to 230 million acre feet of Canadian water could be made available for diversion.

The idea that great surpluses exist when water is not being directly consumed or used in some economic way by people is basic to the proposals of most water export advocates. The calculations are as simplistic as those we have seen used to project "need" in the United States. Dr. Laycock, for instance, suggests that the export of one or two per cent of Canada's water could be undertaken, while the Hon. Alvin Hamilton would go as high as 6 or 7 per cent. In fact, however, proposals that various percentages of the total Canadian water supply might be made available for exports are meaningless. It is not statistical amounts of total water inventories that are dammed and diverted, it is living rivers and the manipulation of them that is involved. A small percentage of Canada's water could be a sufficiently large part of the flow of one or more rivers to have devastating social and environmental effects.

It is obvious, then, that discussion of abstract amounts of water that might be considered surplus implies a complete misunderstanding of the role of rivers and lakes as part of a living landscape. The amount of water per capita in Canada is large in comparison to per capita quantities in the U.S., but this obvious fact is totally irrelevant to the question of presence or absence of surplus. As Dr. A. T. Prince, Director of Inland Waters for the Department of the Environment in Ottawa, puts it: "The water supply in Canada is very great — it's large in proportion to our population but it's about average for the area of the country as compared to other parts of the world. It is not a great surplus in relation to our geographic size."

Dr. Frank Quinn of the Department of the Environment, Ottawa, points out the need to qualify the commonly made assertion that Canada has 25 to 40 percent of the world's fresh surface water. Such figures refer to accumulated storage in the Great Lakes and other large and small lakes in the north. The amount of water that is actual runoff and therefore to be considered in any discussion of export is just 6 per cent of the world's runoff. Furthermore, Canada is not nearly so fortunate as countries such as the United States which have (or had) enormous underground fresh water sources. With vast areas dominated by perma-frost or rock, Canada probably has much less than her share of groundwater.

Geographer Trevor Lloyd of McGill University elaborated on this in the July 1970 issue of *Foreign Affairs*. "The landscape of much of the far north includes a rich variety of lakes, ponds and rivers and gives an impression of providing a reserve of water which might become available for use elsewhere. The impression is misleading. Precipitation over much of the north is low, although evaporation is also low, and the perma-frost beneath prevents the water from draining away. While information is still incomplete, it suggests that the northern water reserves can contribute little or nothing for export southward."

No "surplus" of Canadian water has yet been established, and whether any will be identified becomes increasingly doubtful with our deepening understanding of the nature of water, and as the consequences of manipulating rivers becomes more obvious. And so it becomes increasingly irresponsible to speak of the export or diversion of any percentage of Canadian water without clearly defining what water is involved, and providing evidence that water in specific rivers is clearly surplus to their environmental, social, and economic needs. Any claims of surplus Canadian water presented in a less definitive way must be considered specious and worthy of no consideration.

It is interesting to note the shifting nature of Canadian opposition to export of water. Not long ago, it was based on a feeling that water would be the basis of great economic growth in Canada, and that exporting water would be exporting the possibility of industrial expansion. General A. G. L. McNaughton was a champion of that viewpoint. In an address of the Canadian Club in Montreal in October, 1965, he said: "In Canada, the upper limit of development is high in great part because of our water resources. This fact should be an inducement for us to speed up our progress rather than to relinquish the fundamental asset that makes it possible. It is therefore nonsense to talk about a surplus and it is dangerous folly even to contemplate selling water. All our water can be translated into growth somewhere. Let this growth take place in Canada."

General McNaughton was fiercely nationalistic, an emotion that was looked upon with some suspicion in that era when continentalism was the approach to relations with the United States commonly adopted by those Canadians who considered themselves sophisticated in international affairs. For instance, the prestigious Western Canadian-American assembly, meeting in August of 1964 at Harrison Hot Springs, British Columbia, under the sponsorship of the University of British Columbia and New York's Columbia University, made the following statement:

Canada and the United States are moving in the direction of a new and significant policy for the development of energy resources, particularly water power, on a continental scale. Recent technological advances which have made the border increasingly irrelevant have brought about in both countries a willingness to consider an encouraging degree of integration.

This was also the general viewpoint of the Merchant-Heeney Report drawn up in 1965 for the Canadian and American governments by Livingston Merchant, former American Ambassador to Canada, and by Arnold Heeney, former Canadian ambassador to the United States. Significantly, Heeney was the man who followed General McNaughton as chairman of the Canadian section of the International Joint Commission. This report, published in 1967, not only supported a continental view of Canadian energy and water development, but strongly recommended that discussions of such matters be carried on by the two nations behind closed doors. In the words of the report:

Many problems between our two governments are susceptible of solution only through the quiet, private and patient examination of facts in the search for accommodation. It should be regarded as incumbent on both parties during this time-consuming process to avoid, so far as possible, the

*adoption of public division and difference. . . . Canadian
authorities must be satisfied that the practice of quiet
diplomacy is not only neighbourly and convenient to the
United States but that is is in fact more effective than the
alternative of raising a row and being unpleasant in public.*

Of course, quiet diplomacy can benefit only the larger
and more powerful participant. There is an endless list of
pressures that the United States could apply in secret negotiations that would be untenable in public discussions. Such
would undoubtedly be the case in any energy and water
negotiations that might be undertaken between our two nations in the secretive manner endorsed by the Merchant-
Heeney Report, and that appears to be commonly practised
in U.S.-Canadian relations today.

Prof. E. Kuiper has stated that export from one country to
another would only be feasible if, "during the foreseeable
future, the exporting as well as the importing country should
be able to maintain bargaining positions of nearly equal
strength, so that treaty adjustments from period to period
can be made, without disrupting the economy of one of the
countries, and without disturbing the existing goodwill that
was created in the first place." The existence of such a relationship between two nations of which one is ten times the
economic size and power of the other is questionable at the
very least. So too is the proposition put forth by Professor
Kuiper and Dr. Laycock, among others, suggesting that contracts for the sale of Canadian water to the United States
could be renegotiated as to quantity and price every 25 years.
U.S. Senator Frank Moss of Utah has put it quite succinctly.
"If the [Canadian] water were diverted and being sold and
if industry and life came to depend on that source of supply,
obviously then to cut it off would cause such a cataclysmic
change that it would be all but unthinkable." Or as Edward
Weinberg, legal advisor in the U.S. Department of the Interior has said: "No realistic plan for large-scale diversion
would be economically and socially justifiable if it did not
assure that, in view of the large costs involved and the plans
made in reliance on such supplies, there was an assured supply for a very long period of time."

Mr. Weinberg has also pointed up what to many Canadians is one of the crucial issues in water export. "The nature
of discussions between sovereign nations gives a quality to
any studies and negotiations vastly different than that in

domestic situations where ultimately one sovereign has authority to enact a law for the water resource." What form would the necessary administration of an international water system take? Would some sort of international body be established for the purpose? Acceptance of this by Canadians would be highly unlikely, and even proponents of export oppose "supra-national" control. Any suggestion that the International Joint Commission study the question of export has been firmly rejected since it would require this U.S.-Canadian body to examine water resources that are totally Canadian. But though formal international authority over Canadian rivers would not be accepted in Canada, U.S. control would be quite complete over any water resources involved in export. This would be implicit in any export contract regardless of wording, since of course the purpose of it would be to provide the water at the times and in the quantities desired by the U.S.

The Columbia River Treaty is held to be an admirable example of international cooperation by many export supporters. In that case, operational co-operation simply amounts to the U.S. stating how much water it wants to cross the border in the Columbia river at a given time, and the Canadian authorities turn the taps accordingly. Yet Canadian apologists for the Columbia treaty insist that Canada controls the river.

Most advocates of export of Canadian water clearly state that they would only support such a program if it were in the economic interests of Canada to do so. Dr. John Hare, past president of the Canadian Water Resources Association, says: "Obviously we should be looking at all aspects of marketing products that we have available in this country, particularly if it will bring in necessary dollars that we need to develop our country in other ways. One of the things that we do have in this world is a large supply of the total water, and as such it should be a marketable commodity for Canadians." Of the water export issue, Prof. E. Kuiper of the University of Manitoba states: "I think that question is very similar as to should we export coal, should we export oil, should we export anything. If it is profitable to us I do not see any reason why we should not."

Such a view is quite in keeping with the economic development of Canada since this nation was set on a course of deliberate integration into the multi-national corporate fold, beginning in the 1940's under the guidance of the Hon. C.D.

Howe. Without that philosophy it would have taken Canadians longer to achieve their present standard of living. But as the Canadian philosopher Professor George Grant has said: "The society produced by such policies may reap enormous benefits, but it will not be a nation. Its culture will become the empire's to which it belongs. Branch plant economies have branch-plant cultures. . . . When everything is made relative to profit-making, all traditions of virtue are dissolved, including that aspect of virtue known as love of country." A water policy based primarily on profit could carry within it enormous costs for this nation. Canadians must face the total long range implications of such a policy.

The concept of continental resource development, particularly of energy and water, no longer enjoys the level of popular approval prevalent in 1964 at the time of signing the Columbia River Treaty. Many Canadians are now more disposed to listen to the words of men such as the nation's most eminent historian, Donald Creighton, who sees continentalism threatening the foundations upon which Canada has been built. "The purposes of the Fathers [of Confederation] were political and social as well as economic. Their primary object had been the establishment of a separate British-American nation and an independent northern economy based on a trans-continental east-west axis."

It will be shown how the natural flow of Canadian water could hardly be better designed to further that end. Conversely, diversion of Canadian water southward would be the greatest single step toward continentalism that could be envisioned. The rivers whose flow was a vital factor in the creation of an independent Canada would be transformed into permanent physical ties with the U.S.

Professor Creighton suggests: "Continentalism has divorced Canadians from their history, crippled their creative capacity, and left them without the power to fashion a new future for themselves." Almost all of our energy resources are now controlled by foreign corporations. Water is the last great resource still owned by Canadians. Its integration into a North American system would make the current domination by multi-national corporations almost seem a nationalistic influence by comparison.

There are those Canadians who suggest that if Canada does not agree to some sort of water export to the United States, pressure of such an extreme nature could be initiated that we would have little choice in the matter. But as we have seen the "water crisis" is largely political in nature. it is not likely therefore that the U.S. could ever mount a sustained campaign based on "need" for Canadian water. In fact, some Americans, such as Senator Henry Jackson of the state of Washington, Chairman of the powerful Senate Interior and Insular affairs committee, have rejected the idea of their country even making overtures to Canada. "Any matter relating to the use of Canadian water ought to emanate from Canada. I don't think it's proper for Americans to talk about getting water from Canada unless the Canadians raise the question. After all, Canada's a sovereign, free and independent country and I respect that." It should be noted that Senator Jackson, while quite probably motivated to some extent by respect for Canada, may be even more inclined to this view as a means of protecting his own region, the Pacific Northwest.

It's interesting that the same fear of the Southwest that causes Senator Jackson to oppose U.S. initiatives leading to Canadian water importation has led others in his region to support Canadian water importation. Probably they consider the diversion of the Columbia inevitable and want to have replacement water on tap. In any case, the real importance of Senator Jackson's stand and that of other Americans who share his views is that it makes a U.S.-Canadian confrontation on the issue less likely — if Canada takes a firm stand on the export issue. Some Americans hope in fact this happens soon. Says economist James Crutchfield: "I think the major thing it would do immediately is to force the United States to a recognition that it must make more efficient use of the water already available to it. I'm very much afraid of the lingering relief mechanism that is in the minds of millions of Americans that if somehow we manage to mess up our own water supply so badly that it really hurts our economic welfare, we can always count on the abundant Canadian supplies to bail us out, even though we may have to pay a fairly handsome price for it."

Or as ecologist Dr. Paul Ehrlich of Stanford University says: "The very best thing that Canadians could do for the United States as far as water exportation is concerned is that they say right now, absolutely and forever, not one drop of water will cross the American border."

As we have seen opposition by Canadians to the idea of export of Canadian water originally was based on political and economic grounds. More recently, however, opposition to export has been swinging around to stress the environmental deterioration that water export could involve. Sale of Canadian water means dams and diversions and flooded valleys and manipulated rivers and drowned waterfalls. Canadians, and Americans too, are becoming deeply concerned as the evidence piles up of the horrendous damage resulting from water development, whether or not it involves political boundaries.

And so in addition to the economic and political questions, we are now seeing a new form of nationalism which questions water export because of its effect on Canada as a natural entity. It is clear, as we will discuss in chapter 9, that Canada is a product of its land, and dependent upon the integrity of that land for survival. It is also clear that few actions of man have a more profound and immediate effect upon the land and the water which gives it life than water development. This resurgence of a nationalism anchored in the soil and water of Canada, seems destined to meet head-on the philosophy of those who are promoting water development within Canada's borders, as well as the continentalism of those who advocate export of the nation's water. There is growing resistance to the idea of converting the natural water courses of the nation into a gigantic plumbing system.

Evidence of this new attitude is to be found in every province. It is generally agreed that at least in part the former Conservative Government of Manitoba was defeated by a public aroused over plans to dam the Churchill River and divert its flow to the Nelson, flooding the thousand square miles of Southern Indian Lake and displacing the Indians who depended upon it for their livelihood. In Alberta, "PRIME is a Crime" bumper stickers expressed the attitude of many Albertans towards water development. Their concern was reflected in the shelving of the PRIME (Prairie Rivers Improvement, Management, and Evaluation) program when the provincial government changed hands in the election of 1971. In British Columbia, opposition to a proposed dam at Moran Canyon on the Fraser has become one of the biggest issues in the province, while in Northern Ontario a "Damn the Dams" movement has arisen in the wake of federal-provincial diversion studies in that province.

Much of this concern is based upon the social and environmental impact of water development. Add to that the growing forces of economic and political nationalism, and a recognition in Canada that American "need" is the result of bad management in some cases, indefensible economics in most cases, and a policy that promotes endless growth at whatever cost. With all this, proposals for water export can be assured of a rough ride in Canada.

Recognition of these changing attitudes have caused proponents of export to react with some bitterness. Geographer Dr. Arleigh Laycock described as a "hang-up" in thinking about water export something he calls "the new ecology." "The more extreme ecologist can see nothing but destruction and devastation in our past, and gloom and doom in our future. Any kind of development is bad and we must all return to nature." This has been in general the reaction of the more extreme advocates of water development in both the United States and Canada to the deepening concern among citizens of both countries as evidence mounts of the devastating effect of most of our more recent water developments.

Opponents of water export in Canada are usually characterized by export enthusiasts as being emotional or even hysterical. Soon after its election, the new Conservative government of Alberta stated its opposition to any consideration of water export, and stopped the PRIME project studies. The Lethbridge *Herald*, long a supporter of water development and export, commented: "The new Alberta government is altogether too sensitive, too emotional, in the matter of water development. The election is over. The Conservatives can now afford to be calmer and more responsible in their policy statements." The newspaper's publisher, Cleo Mowers, earlier told the American National Water Resources Association in Las Vegas: "Canadians, on balance, are as mature and reasonable as Americans, and reason in this matter [of water export] will eventually replace hysteria. This process of our return to reason you can facilitate but you cannot hurry."

It is interesting to note that much of the support for Canadian water export originates in the prairie provinces. In fact, the Canadian Water Resources Association, the country's loudest drum-beater for water export, was until a few years ago the Western Canadian Reclamation Association. Its major support came from the irrigated areas of southern Alberta, and this is where great support for water development and export still seems to thrive. This is understandable, since it is a region which has prospered on irrigated agriculture. A fairly representative point of view of the region was that expressed by Dr. C.C. Stewart, President of Lethbridge Community College, in addressing the annual convention of the Agricultural Institute of Canada in July, 1971:

For the next decade, let our policy on water development be changed from:
Canada is blessed with an abundance of good, clean water, more water than any other country in the world. We must protect it.
to:
Canada is blessed with an abundance of good, clean water. Let us develop it.

Of course, such an unsophisticated view of water policy would not be put forward today by even a development-oriented dam-building agency, but it is an honest localized view that has many followers in Canada. It has an attractive simplicity unencumbered by complicating factors such as economics or ecology.

Fortunately, although Canada has not yet evolved a long range water policy, the federal government has reached the point where R.J. Orange, MP, parliamentary secretary to the Minister of Energy, Mines and Resources, could say in 1970: "We do not believe in development merely for the sake of development. . . . Decisions must be based upon a careful examination of sociological, economic and ecological factors as well as mere technical feasibility." As we have seen, this sort of thinking is far from being generally applied in Canada as yet. It is clear, however, that the case for water development for its own sake can no longer be taken seriously in Canada. Yet, many projects under study or construction indicate that water development per se is still strongly believed in and promoted as being for the public good.

Agriculturists and others who have seen the benefits of local water development quite naturally extend their support of projects involving relatively small amounts of water for local irrigation programs, into enthusiasm for much larger inter-basin transfer schemes within Canada's borders. And from there it's not such a big step to acceptance of the concept of water export to the United States. Why should a good neighbour deny the benefits he enjoys to an American just because he lives on the other side of an invisible border?

Canada's water: for sale?   47

Why not help make the desert 1000 miles south "bloom like a rose"?

But there is of course a vast difference between spilling the waters of a river over its banks for a local irrigation project, and restructuring whole systems of rivers to ship large quantities of water enormous distances. Quite apart from the politics and economics involved, such projects are not just "more of the same". They are different in nature, and "experience with small-scale development does not necessarily provide all the necessary answers to large-scale development," as Jay M. Bagley of Utah State University has said. The reasons for this will become apparent as we examine in detail the economic, environmental and social aspects of large-scale water transfers. This is of course quite apart from the political questions already discussed.

Finally, those Canadians who advocate the export of water usually suggest that water is an unending renewable resource that we can sell and it is replaced by nature perpetually. Many suggest that is it preferable to sell water rather than such non-renewable resources as oil and gas which can be developed and sold but once.

Water as a "renewable resource" is a quite misleading argument, because regardless of the terminology used, what is sold under long term and essentially permanent treaty is not a quantity of water, but rather a proportion of a river. If Canada is committed to sell so many acre feet each year, it has essentially lost for any relevant time span the proportion of the affected river which that amount of water represents. Since we no longer would have the option of deciding to use the water in an alternative way, it cannot be classed as a renewable resource such as trees, which after cutting may be replaced by new trees, and new decisions made about their use.

The advocacy of the sale of water as a resource "like any other" reveals a profound misunderstanding of the role of water in the landscape. Oil or gas can usually be sold without affecting permanently the land under which it lies—although this is untrue in much of Canada's north. But water is an integral part of the land, responsible to a large extent for its physical form and the life found in or near it—including man. The land and water are indivisible, and those who would treat a river as so much plumbing to be manipulated, and its water as a commodity to be bought and sold like carloads of wheat, have simply not comprehended this fundamental fact.

Nor does this view of water as a marketable resource add up for economists such as Dr. S. E. Drugge of the University of Alberta. "The attitude taken by some that water is just another natural resource to be allocated and sold at a profit-producing price, seems to me to be in serious error. The fundamental mistake in this approach to allocating water on the basis of the market mechanism, is that this natural resource is fundamentally and inextricably co-extensive and co-existent with our national economy and therefore standard of living, and indeed our standard of life. That is to say, if we apply the reasoning that northern water should be allocated to the highest bidder at home or abroad, then why shouldn't we similarly calculate which portions of this country's land mass is 'surplus to our need,' and sell these land masses to the highest bidder."

In summary, then, there seems no clearly definable official Canadian attitude on the question of water export to the United States. Government statements are sufficiently hedged, and the unofficial views of government spokesmen have been so varied, that it does not seem possible to accept with any real confidence official statements that Canadian water is not for sale.

The viewpoint of Canadians generally has not yet crystallized, although a majority quite clearly opposes export. But as it becomes recognized that no real need exists in the United States for Canadian water, as evidence accumulates of the great environmental price paid in most large water developments, as the strange economics of the water industry becomes better known, and with a rising tide of Canadian nationalism based at least to some extent on the integrity of the land, Canadian opinion appears to be swinging even further away from any possibility of favourable consideration of water export. How effectively this is translated into public policy will be a measure of Canada's political maturity, and a crucial factor in its survival as a nation.

Chapter 4
The real costs of dam building

Bay D'Espoir, Mactaquac, Manicouagan, Kettle Rapids, Gardiner, Big Horn, Bennett . . .

Oroville, Hoover, Grand Coulee, Garrison, Kinzua . . .

Aswan, Volta, Kariba, Snowy Mountains, Tarbella, Kogna, Inguri . . .

Dams. Big dams. Canadian dams, American dams, dams around the world. Almost all of them built since the Second World War, for the generation of electrical energy, or for irrigation of dry lands, or for flood control, or for the diversion of water from one river to another.

"Few actions of which man is capable in a similar time and place can have such far-reaching ecological effects — physically, biologically, and socioeconomically — as a major hydroelectric dam. Many of these effects are dynamically irreversible, at least until such time as the dam is removed or abandoned for its primary use. Thus, in many of their aspects, dams and their reservoirs are potentially agents of environmental degradation, be they constructed for hydroelectricity, for one of their other recognized primary uses, or for multipurpose use." These were statements of Dr. Karl F. Lagler of the University of Michigan, speaking at the 1969 annual meeting of the American Association for the Advancement of Science. He added: "Although water power from large dams continues ostensibly to be the cheapest source of electric energy in many parts of the world, it is often cheap only because of the failure of governments fully to reckon the secondary social and ecological costs."

Many of the world's great dams are marvels of engineering. Many of them have been born in controversy. After completion, however, all have been remarkable for an almost total lack of re-assessment by those who built them and those who authorized them. For these agencies are usually deeply involved with the next project, and the one after that, as governments around the world proceed to dam, divert, and in every possible way manipulate their great rivers. The natural water systems have taken millions of years to evolve.

They helped to create and are a part of, the living landscape. In a few decades they are being completely changed to provide power, water and flood protection.

The technology required to build large dams is almost totally of this century, and it is really in the past two decades that the phenomenal rate of big dam construction has occurred. So it's not surprising that only recently has evidence concerning the environmental impact of reservoir construction and water diversion begun to accumulate in quantity, as people outside the dam-building establishment look more closely at what is going on. At the same time, water development projects are growing larger, and the number of them is rocketing in a seeming effort to dam or in some way manipulate every possible river in the shortest possible time. In fact, by 1980 we will, if present plans are followed through, be able to look back on the 1950 to 1980 period as "the decades of the dam builders."

The meaning of this is staggering and it adds up to this: by the time we begin to understand in an organized way the impact of massive dams singly and in multiple structure projects, most of the rivers with development potential will have been dammed, and all our acquired understanding will be merely an academic exercise. It will be clear to everyone by 1980 that we have restructured the major physical and biological entities of North America, and indeed the world, while in a state of comparative ignorance of what we were doing, and in fact while deliberately ignoring the limited knowledge that was available.

It is not necessary to wait until all the studies have been done, all the scientific papers have been published, and all the textbooks written, in order to gain an appreciation of what is happening. Around the world, evidence is accumulating that water developments are providing benefits that are something less than promised, that those benefits are temporary, usually very expensive, and are achieved at a cost of social and environmental repercussions far beyond what was expected. Consider, for example, what is perhaps the most famous instance of this, the High Aswan Dam in Egypt.

The Aswan Dam was to be the proudest achievement of the late Egyptian President Gamal Abdul Nasser. Built with Russian technical and financial assistance, it would provide life-giving water to irrigate 1.3 million acres and to control the annual floods that have always been a part of the annual cycle of the river and its people. Above all, it was to provide the electrical energy that would make Egypt a modern industrial state.

Reality has made a sad travesty of these dreams. The once brown and muddy Nile now flows green and beautiful in the hot sun, and no more does it rampage across the land of the fellahin of Egypt. No more does that annual flood add new fertility to the farmlands of the Nile; instead, the silt that created one of the world's most fertile regions, the Nile Delta, drops to the bottom of the new Lake Nasser, behind the Dam. Sometime in the future — estimates range upward from a century — Lake Nasser will be filled with soil and useless as a reservoir. In the meantime, it is costing Egypt more than one hundred million dollars annually just to pay for the fertilizer that is required to make up for the lost silt.

Instead of 1.3 million acres, just over half, or 750,000 acres, has proven to be suitable for irrigation by water from Aswan. And less than half of that has actually been developed for irrigation. It has provided a five per cent increase in cultivated land in Egypt, during a period when the underfed population of the country grew by one third. For those growing throngs the newly tamed river has brought yet another unforseen legacy: a rapid spread of bilharzia, the ancient disease of the tropics that sometimes kills but more often condemns its victims to a life of pain and exhaustion. It thrives in the snails that like the still waters of reservoirs and irrigation canals, and from them spreads quickly throughout any nearby human population. Where new canals have been dug since the construction of Aswan, up to 80 per cent of the people nearby have become infected. Almost half the population had the disease before Aswan, and it cost the country hundreds of millions of dollars annually in lost production and futile attempts at cures. Millions more Egyptians are now exposed.

Instead of adding soil to the delta, the Nile now cuts away at it; the river no longer carries nutrients into the Mediterranean and Egyptian fishermen have lost a sardine fishery that once ran to 18,000 tons a year. What estimate can be made of the loss to the world as magnificent art treasures of ancient Egypt disappear beneath the waves? What sort of benefits can be expected from a project in which the hot sun and wind evaporates twice as much water from the reservoir as was expected, and out of which the rising water seeps through the porous sandstone of its western banks? The reservoir loses more than a third of the water that flows into it, and instead of being full as planned by 1970, it was not half full in 1972 and one Egyptian authority estimated it might take two hundred years to fill. Professor Paul Ehrlich has suggested only partly in jest that the best hope for Egypt might be that the reservoir either silts up so fast as to be soon useless, or that the Israelis slip in and blow it up!

Sadly, the Aswan experience is not exceptional. In other parts of the tropics, the tragedy has been compounded by the wholesale removal from ancestral lands of many thousands of people. Their presence before the rising waters is often considered a nuisance impeding the industrialization that the dam symbolizes. The power produced is no assurance of a leap into the technological era — for instance, the Egyptians have not yet found a use for more than a third of the energy from Aswan. Many diseases other than bilharzia are fostered by the new reservoirs, and unplanned communities sometimes spring up on the shores of new lakes to take advantage of the flush of fishing that usually follows impoundment. Typically, the fish population quickly falls off, often to lower levels than before damming, and more social problems then are faced. Since many of those displaced may have been subsistence farmers, typically scorned in nations hoping to "take off" into the modern era, the burden that they now place on the remainder of the economy becomes evident only after they have been displaced by flooding, or by having their farming eliminated by the pattern of water releases downstream.

The great dams of the tropics provide a long story of tragedy with few mitigating factors. Several years of studying and reporting on such developments led Washington *Post* writer Claire Sterling to conclude: "Once a giant dam is built, it is *there,* evaporating, transpiring, leaking, silting up or weeding over, scouring the riverbed, driving the fish away or killing them off, drenching or salting the soil, breaking timeless natural laws, banishing people; and every day those turbines stand idle the minister of finance is closer to a nervous breakdown. Because nobody is giving them away. All the rich countries offer is hard currency, technicians, and equipment, on loan, at interest. In the end it is the poor countries who pay, and pay, and pay."

It is ironical that for years American and United Nations experts have been studying the possibility of building the multi-billion-dollar Pa Mong Dam on the Mekong River. The catalogue of losses that such a dam would cause in

South Viet-Nam and Thailand suggests that even the war has been a relatively benign influence in comparison. Well-meaning American "conscience money" spent on the Mekong could be the greatest catastrophe brought by the West to Southeast Asia.

The same sort of reasoning that has led to the disastrous tropical dams has been involved in the construction of North American water developments. The details are different, and Canada and the United States are better able to absorb the cost of these great projects into their economies, and can sometimes come up with technological bandaids to overcome some of the problems, but the general impact is often similar. Consider, for example, the W. A. C. Bennett Dam in British Columbia.

From high in the air the reservoir is a spectacular sight. Its three great arms are rimmed by snow-peaked mountains. Where once the Finlay River flowing south in the Rocky Mountain Trench met the Parsnip River flowing north, a 680 square mile reservoir, Lake Williston, now is the dominant fact of the area. Where once the Peace River provided the only navigable stream through the Rocky Mountains, a gigantic dam 600 feet high, costing about three quarters of a billion dollars, converts the energy of that great river into what is supposed to be cheap hydro-electric power.

Fly lower, though, and it begins to appear that the power may not have been so cheap after all. The reservoir is ugly with great floating masses of timber. Along the shore line the drowning trees stand, and many are slumping, and you know that they will still be there decades hence, gray and hard. Clouds of dust blow from great clay cliffs, which are gradually undercut until another massive slide sends waves up to fifty feet high surging across the lake.

Stand on the Dam, high above the humming turbines, and remember that to produce cheap power 680 square miles of magnificent Canadian wilderness have been obliterated forever. The best of three great rivers, with their highly productive forest lands, all now lie beneath the deep water. Six thousand moose were supported by that land, according to biologist Ken Sumaniuk of Prince George, B.C. Unknown mineral and archaeological sites will never now be found. All were contributed at no cost at all to the project. These were the lands from which the Tall Grass Indians made their living, ranging nomadically with the seasons along the Finlay River. And they were lands which could have provided recreation for thousands of people each year, forever. The drowned land was home for a few white men too, farmers and ranchers and people like Bud Stewart, who took visitors on an exciting trip on the Peace River through the Rocky Mountains. Above all, it was a land of incredible beauty, and now it is ugly. But nobody, and nothing, was important enough to stand in the way of what some called cheap power. Because cheap power was the key to Progress.

Seven hundred miles downstream from the Dam, the Peace River meets the Slave River just below Lake Athabasca. There it helps create one of the nation's most productive wetlands — the one thousand square mile Peace-Athabasca Delta. It consists of many small and some large shallow lakes connected by winding channels, and it is an important staging area for the four major continental flyways of waterfowl during spring and fall migration. It also was home to large numbers of muskrats and was a vital factor in the Lake Athabasca fishery. Some 6,000 bison of Wood Buffalo National Park are also maintained by the Delta.

About 1300 Indians live part of the year at Fort Chipewyan or on their reserve across Lake Athabasca from the town. Many of them spend part of the year along the waterways of the Delta, depending largely on the wildlife of the Delta. But beginning in 1968 when the gates in the Bennett dam far upstream were closed, all this changed. In 1970, thirteen Alberta scientists signed a document they called "Death of a Delta" which outlined what was happening to the wetlands. The facts were presented in more detail at a symposium of scientists at the Peace-Athabasca Delta Symposium held in January of 1971.

It appeared that the Bennett Dam, by preventing the annual spring flood, had stopped a process essential to the life of the Delta. A unique situation existed whereby the spring flood on the Peace created a sort of hydraulic dam when it poured into the Slave River. This forced the water from Lake Athabasca, also pouring into the Slave, back into the Delta. An annual replenishment of water was provided for all the lakes and marshes of the Delta in this way, no matter how low the rivers flowed in years of light precipitation. With the spring floods on the Peace eliminated, the water levels in Lake Athabasca and the Delta had by 1970 dropped several feet. Some of the smaller bodies of water in the Delta had dried up completely, while the larger ones were rapidly shrinking. Waterfowl habitat was greatly reduced in both quantity and quality, and muskrat populations were greatly reduced since the shallow water was freezing down to the bottom of the lakes in winter. This factor was also affecting the fishery, and commercial fishing on Lake Athabasca was expected to collapse within three to five years. The Delta was expected to offer a reduced carrying capacity for bison over the long term, although there would be increased habitat for moose with the changing plant life.

As in most water development, it was the native people of the area who were most seriously affected. The 1,300 Cree, Chipewyan and Metis residents of Fort Chipewyan and region had their main sources of income, the muskrats and the fish, largely eliminated. A dam hundreds of miles away, about which they had not been consulted and from which they would not benefit, had taken from them a livelihood and a way of life. Visiting their camps in the Delta in the summer of 1970, the injustice of the situation was very tangible. The lives of these people, and hundreds of thousands like them around the world, were largely destroyed by distant men in boardrooms making decisions about the water which sustained their lives. They hadn't bothered to consider the people who would really pay for someone else's "cheap power".

In the case of the Indians of the Peace-Athabasca Delta, the facts of the matter were still being denied by the responsible authorities long after they had been clearly spelled out. That the dam could have affected the Delta or its people was denied by Premier W.A.C. Bennett, after whom the dam was named; by his water resources minister after whom the Williston Reservoir was named; and by the Chairman of B.C. Hydro after whom the Gordon Shrum Power House was named. Strangely, the Social Credit Government of Alberta at the time also was anxious to avoid placing any blame for the situation. The reason for this becomes evident, however, when it is realized that the government was promoting its PRIME water development program which would have the effect of reducing still further the water flow of the Athabasca system. It was about to start on the Pembina Dam, west of Edmonton. The Pembina River is a tributary of the Athabasca, and damming it would undoubtedly aggravate the problems of the Delta caused by the damming of the Peace. A change of government in Alberta in 1971 brought these plans to at least a temporary halt.

These two examples, one foreign and one Canadian, have been discussed in some detail in order to provide some insight into the kinds of complications that are to be found in water development generally. It should be noted that neither the Aswan nor the Bennett dams diverted water away from the natural course of its river. The complications arose through controlling the flow of the river. That is just the first step, the first set of ecological and sociological complications which could be expected in water diversions such as would be required in the export of Canadian water to the United States; or in diversions within Canada as are planned in the PRIME or Saskatchewan-Nelson Basin schemes, or the northern Ontario diversions or the James Bay project in Quebec or the Churchill-Nelson hydro diversion in Manitoba. Such programs would provide a much more complicated situation by completely or partly removing water from some rivers and adding to others; and by operating whole systems of dams and diversions together.

It is clear that the water development we have carried out in the past, and the projects we expect to construct in the future have been the result of a quite complete misunderstanding of the nature of rivers and lakes and all the forms of life associated with them. There is no major water development in Canada in which environmental considerations have played a significant role in decision making, or where social factors other than "man as consumer" played any part. A few perfunctory studies were made in some cases after the decisions were made. Public relations releases explained the great care that would be taken "to preserve and enhance the ecology," and how displaced persons would be better off than ever before. Any serious discussion of water development is concerned with rates of flow, rates of consumption, kilowatt hours of energy, tons of concrete, feet of aqueduct, yards of earth fill, acre feet of water, interest rates on borrowed money. It is on the basis of the manipulation of such readily measurable elements that water development proceeds.

In short, water development decisions are made as if rivers were simply pipes carrying water to the sea. Pipes into which taps and elbows and branches and extensions could be added as long as enough water kept flowing in them, and as long as some sort of salesmanship and financial manoeuvering made it possible to sell the idea of all those fixtures to the public.

Of course, rivers and streams are not like that at all, and

manipulating them as if they were can only be disastrous. Alberta biologist Dennis MacDonald puts it this way: "Rivers are extremely complex. They involve a total biological system that has evolved over millions of years, and it is this complex web of life, this inter-relationship between the vegetation along the river and the organisms within the river itself that is often damaged severely by man's activity." The hydrologists point out that rivers are dynamic systems that carry loads of sediment, deposit it, erode banks, build up shorelines, change course and speed in answer to immutable laws of physics. Dr. Luna Leopold, one of the world's greatest authorities on rivers, states that when man dams and diverts rivers: "Erosion and sedimentation will not be restricted to the place that the engineering work occurs. In those long river basins you can have the detrimental effects spread for hundreds or thousands of miles downstream . . . and also possibly upstream."

Rivers create, and are created by, the landscape through which they flow. As they begin in the highlands, their relationship with the land is complete, and they receive silt and minerals from the rock and soil over which they flow. Food for the fish and other forms of life drops from the trees and bushes and plants along its banks. Remove the trees in careless logging or construction activities, and the fish too are removed; disturb the rocky spawning beds and the fish, some of which may be salmon migrating hundreds of miles from the sea, cannot lay eggs. Dam the river, and the silt it carries drops to the bottom, gradually filling in the reservoir until, perhaps in the lifetime of a man, perhaps in two centuries, it fills up and the dam becomes little more than a waterfall. Much will have been sacrificed to that end.

Downstream of the dam, the clear-running water tries to pick up its load again, and scours the banks, eroding them at a much faster rate and perhaps seriously affecting bridge supports, farmlands, settlements, and any other river bank use. If the dam has been built as part of a diversion, water from one river will be poured into another. The much greater volume of water will erode banks, eliminate by its speed the resting places for trout and other fish and organisms that evolved over centuries. The erosion of stream-bank vegetation will effect wildlife populations along the length of the river. It is now a sluiceway, with as much life and beauty as the term suggests.

A good example of such scouring and erosion is to be seen

in the stream down which large volumes of water from the Ogoki diversion in Northern Ontario rushes toward Lake Superior by way of Lake Nipigon. The diversion was completed in the early nineteen forties, and still great clouds of silt are carried far out into the lake. The source of the material can be seen along the length of the stream where raw, eroded clay banks and toppling trees mark the undercutting of the banks by the excessive flow of water. Buzz Taisy operates a fishing resort on Lake Nipigon, and he describes what happened: "Up in Ombobika Bay (where the diverted water enters Lake Nipigon) it's just silted right in ... there were good pickerel beds up there where they were spawning ... You can go up there now and you might as well stay out of the bay, because it's just ... muddy, dirty water."

Water temperature is altered by dams, both within the reservoir and downstream of it. So is the chemistry of the water — in the reservoir, there may be deep zones totally lacking in oxygen, and in these depths hydrogen sulfide may be produced. This may be reflected downstream, where the river or a lake may no longer support fish life. It has been suggested that chemical change within the Duncan Reservoir in British Columbia has been responsible for large fish kills showing up downstream in Kootenay Lake.

At the other end of Kootenay Lake, the Kootenay River flows into it after being impounded by the Libby Dam. Within months of closing the dam, large fish kills were observed in the river from supersaturated nitrogen in the water. Water passing through the sluice gates plunging deep into the river forces air, consisting mainly of nitrogen, into solution. Fish in the water suffer from what deep-sea divers would call "the bends". This condition is an extremely serious problem on the Columbia River, which in the United States is an almost continuous chain of reservoirs from Canada to the ocean.

As a stream becomes a river and approaches the sea, it is the product of perhaps a thousand brooks. It carries within it the life of the great expanse of country which gave it birth. It now is a dominant force in the creation of the landscape. It may build a great delta with the silt it has carried within it over the centuries. The fertile valley of the Fraser River is a magnificent example, stretching one hundred miles from Hope to the sea.

The forms of life within the river become more complex as

fish species increase in number toward its mouth, and as salt-water organisms advance upward into it. The blending of fresh and salt waters creates one of the world's most incredibly productive regions — the estuary. It is thought that 80 per cent of man's total harvest from the sea is dependent at some stage of life on this meeting of water from the sea and water from the land, and on the saltwater marshes that thrive there. Unfortunately, it is precisely at this point that man builds his cities and creates his industry, a tendency that strikes directly at one of his richest sources of food from both sea and land as he pollutes and dredges and paves and prospers. Building dams upstream will eliminate the natural freshets of the river, prevent the seasonal ebb and flow: and the complex relationships of the estuaries will be further changed. Research has only begun to identify the full extent and implication of such changes; so far, says Dr. Peter Larkin of the University of British Columbia, all we can be sure of is that there are indeed a large number of ecological changes downstream from a dam.

A subject of wonder since man walked the land of North America has been the miracle of the salmon with their migration from distant ocean depths up rivers and streams hundreds of miles to the spawning beds where they were born. One of nature's noblest creatures and finest human foods, the salmon has been largely eliminated from many of its most productive rivers on both of the continent's coasts by water development projects, and by pollution. Observation of such rivers as the Columbia and the research of the nation's leading fisheries biologists show clearly that it is not possible to have both salmon and major water developments on the same rivers. But at the moment, the greatest salmon river of them all, the Fraser, is threatened by the dam builders of B.C. Hydro, and by those who see great dams as essential to protect the Fraser Valley from floods. It is likely that other rivers — the Skeena, and the Stikine, for instance — are also being considered for hydro development.

No one knows in detail the effects downstream of diversion of northward-flowing rivers, whether for one of the water export schemes, or for an all-Canadian diversion program. But some scientists have suggested the sort of thing that might be looked for. Dr. Herman Dirschl of the Canadian Wildlife Service led the studies that revealed the extent of damage to the Peace-Athabasca Delta from the Bennett Dam on the Peace River. He suggests: "Sustained low flow levels in the rivers from which water is removed would probably result in a lowering of the permanent ground water table along the river valley which would possibly reduce flows in springs and smaller streams, and lower the water levels of bogs and marshes over a much wider adjoining area. Vegetation patterns would adjust to the drier soil conditions, and the wildlife habitat and populations would consequently be affected. Long-term consequences of large-scale diversions from the Peace and Athabasca rivers would be a significant permanent lowering of the levels of Lake Athabasca, Great Slave Lakes, and the MacKenzie River. Such changes would affect fisheries and would also interfere with navigation along the northern rivers — which it is in the national interest to maintain. The MacKenzie River and its tributaries carry suspended mineral matter and latent heat northward. In fact, the relatively luxuriant vegetation growing in the valley of the MacKenzie exists because the river is there. Were its flow significantly reduced, the associated ecology would become less productive."

Dr. J.P. Bruce, Director of the Canada Centre for Inland Waters at Burlington, Ontario, sees such diversions raising questions of global importance. "The fresh water flowing into the Arctic Ocean from the major rivers of the USSR and Canada contribute to reducing the salinity of Arctic seawater. It is suggested that if substantial volumes of these waters were diverted, the salinity would increase, thus decreasing the amount of ice that forms on the Arctic Ocean. The additional open water would likely then contribute to increased atmospheric water vapour and likely increased snowfall on the land areas of the continents. It is generally thought that this is the kind of triggering mechanism which nature has used over the millennia, to induce a new ice age. Could man then inadvertently start a major climatic change?"

The effects upstream of water development, whether the dam is for hydro power or for consumption or for diversion, has been more clearly recorded and more adequately studied. Typically, Canadian reservoirs are like that on the Brazeau River in Alberta — uncleared of trees, they are dangeous and ugly, with the grey spars of drowned forests standing for decades, and the shores piled and matted with washed-up logs and debris. One of the most tragic examples was the destruction in the 1950's of the world's greatest circular recreational waterway in Tweedsmuir Park in British Columbia. Where once canoes could travel in a three hundred mile circuit of lakes and rivers in a setting of unimaginable mountain beauty, now the stark grey skeletons of the drowned forest make passage dangerous for even heavy power boats with skilled operators. More than a million acres were deleted from the park to put the demeaned lakes outside its boundaries. Even the economic advantages of the destruction proved ephemeral, for aluminum companies no longer find "cheap" hydro power at remote locations a sound investment.

It is incorrect to refer to the reservoir behind a dam as a "lake". The shoreline established over long years by a natural lake has no counterpart in a reservoir. Its great fluctuations in depth — as much as 150 feet in the Mica Reservoir on the Columbia River — means that shore lines are often muddy, debris-laden slopes and flats, useless for any kind of recreational activities. When first filled, the reservoir will likely enjoy a flush of fish production due to the additional nutrients supplied by submerged soil and vegetation. But soon the fishery recedes to normal or below normal production and often the more valuable fish of the river are replaced by less desirable species.

Three B.C. government scientists have described the losses in valleys flooded by water development projects. "Fine beaches go under water, the best parts of spawning streams disappear and cause subsequent reduction of sport fish numbers, wintering grounds of big game species which are hunted in the fall suffer similarly in drop of numbers, specific fur-bearers and other shore animals lose almost completely the essential habitat, and the original foreshore beauty often in large part disappears. Arguments concerning artificial restoration of lost values, while they may be offered as comfort to the bereft, rarely impress those whose training and livelihood keep them in constant touch with specific natural resources. When the climax environment for plant and animal species is violently upset, the work of centuries may be undone and usually there are no restoratives short of the slow changes brought by an equal number of centuries."

The greatest violence possible of course to the natural systems we have been discussing would be completely to cut off the flow of a river and divert it elsewhere. This is precisely what is planned for the Churchill River in Northern Manitoba. About 250 miles from its mouth at Hudson Bay, the Churchill widens into Southern Indian Lake. From the air it looks in many ways like a larger version of Lake of the Woods in Northern Ontario, one of the continent's greatest recreational lakes. It is dotted with islands, and crescent beaches mark much of the shoreline. The movement of water through the lake has created conditions that encourage marine life, and the fishery of the lake made the Indians of the village of South Indian Lake among the most self-reliant in Canada. Some thirty-five fish camps dot the shores and islands of the lakes, and until the plans of Manitoba Hydro were revealed there seemed nothing but prosperity ahead for the Indians living off the unpolluted waters of Southern Indian Lake.

What Hydro has in mind is very simple. At its outlet, the lake spills over Missy Falls, and once again becomes the Churchill River for its last 250 mile run to the sea. A dam would be placed at this outlet, completely drying up that 250 miles of river except for a surge of flood water each spring. Some water would also be contributed by tributaries downstream from the dam. The plug in the river will cause Southern Indian Lake to rise, flooding over its banks and across the permafrost landscape that surrounds it. It is expected that as the permafrost melts the land will quite literally dissolve and slump into the lake, which will become a mass of floating debris. The lake will rise high enough to spill the entire flow of the Churchill across country to the Nelson. The Rat and Burntwood Rivers will virtually disappear. Their valleys will become sluiceways for this great flow of water which will in places spread out 75 miles in width, carrying with it the silt and debris of the dissolving permafrost. The water will empty into the Nelson, already becoming a string of debris-laden reservoirs. For decades, its drowned forests and islands will be marked by the stark gray spars that are a hallmark of Canadian water development.

The Churchill and the Nelson Rivers provide what might be thought of as linear oases through the permafrost and muskeg of Northern Manitoba. The best of the province's northland, where life of all kinds, including human, is richest and most diverse, is to be found along these two rivers. The high land, with its muskeg and permafrost and black spruce swamps is not comparable with the river valley land, and the thousands of more or less stagnant lakes are not nearly as productive or attractive or habitable as the rivers and lakes that are part of the flowing water of the Nelson and Churchill watershed. So it is not just a couple of long thin strips through the north that are to be sacrificed on the altar of "cheap" hydro-electric power. The best of the northern landscape, the parts that hold promise for the future, will no longer exist, nor will the plant and animal life dependent upon the rivers. A single, irrevocable decision will have destroyed a huge section of Canada, and along with it the way of life of a proud and independent group of people.

Manitoba Hydro has made that decision, and the government of Premier Edward Schreyer seems ready to go along with it. This is puzzling, because it is generally recognized that the Schreyer government was at least in part elected on a platform that included a reconsideration of the Churchill diversion. All that has changed from the vigorously opposed plan of the former Conservative government is that a lower level of flooding is now being proposed. This is essentially a meaningless gesture since the first few feet of higher water will be responsible for by far the greatest part of the damage. And the Indians of Southern Indian Lake are sure that a lower level of flooding will be only the first step. They expect that if any flooding occurs, a much greater depth will eventually be developed.

The James Bay Project of the Government of Quebec is similar in many respects to the Manitoba project. It shares the distinction of having its major decisions made with no environmental or sociological considerations. Quebec plans to proceed with the damming and diversion of the five major rivers draining from 144,000 square miles of Quebec into James Bay. The rivers involved are the Nottaway, Broadback, Rupert, Eastmain, and La Grande, and they drain one quarter of the province. They also are the crucially important part of the landscape in which six to seven thousand Indians live. Like those of Southern Indian Lake in Manitoba, they are much more independent of modern technological society than are most Canadian Indians, and they ask to be left alone.

Dr. J.A. Spence of McGill University has put it this way: "The most serious impact of the proposed development will be the almost genocidal destruction of the way of life of the Cree Indians, not only by sociological disruption of their way of life, but by a total disruption of the environment on which these people depend. They cannot survive without lakes, marshes, forests, furbearing animals, moose and game fish. The animals are going to be decimated. Four thousand square miles of forest and many tens of thousands of miles of productive shoreline will be drowned."

"The James Bay project has been conceived and designed as if the Cree Indians did not exist," writes Montreal author Boyce Richardson. And in Montreal, what is about to happen in the James Bay area is with increasing frequence being termed "genocide." It's an ugly word, yet by definition it fits what will be the inevitable result of the project. Richardson reports that throughout the region to be affected, Indians of all ages repeat: "We are thinking about the animals. If you destroy the land, you destroy the animals, and if you destroy the animals, you destroy the Indians. Money? We do not want money. Jobs? How long will these jobs last? Money and jobs are impermanent. They disappear. They do not last. When they are gone the land will still be there. If the land is not destroyed, we can return to it, live off it as we have always done. That is the only way we know how to live."

At James Bay, as at South Indian Lake in Manitoba, the Indians know how small their chances of a satisfying way of life will be in competing with unemployed white men after they have been forced out of their more traditional ways of life. As Basil Colomb says: "We're fighting for our own here, you understand . . . we don't want anyone to flood this lake." In northern Ontario, along the Albany and other rivers which are to be dammed, diverted, and obliterated if the lines on the maps of the planners become reality, the Indians know that it will be they once again who will pay for the white man's war against nature. They remember the fate of the Indians of the Peace-Athabasca Delta in Northern Alberta. Or of the Indians of the valleys flooded by the Bennett Dam in British Columbia. In the United States, water development has been one of the most devastating influences on the Indians of that nation, and the same is becoming true in Canada. For the small bits of land that our natives have been allowed to remain on are invariably in the river valleys. That is where living is best, if you are dependent upon the land.

Life of all kinds, including human, has always been found at its richest and most varied along the rivers and around the lakes. Lewis Mumford has pointed out that the great civilizations of the world have developed in river valleys. "We think of the River Nile and Alexandria; the Tiber and Rome, the Seine and Paris; and so on." Mumford shows too that almost every "Utopia" formulated in the minds of men searching for a better society has been located in a river valley.

Since the marriage of land and water is complete, one cannot be changed without affecting the other. As we proceed with our huge water development plans we are sacrificing much of the best of our wilderness, our wild rivers and lakes, our valleys, and the wildlife and farms and towns sheltered by them. The hundreds of farmers of the St. John Valley in New Brunswick are displaced for, it is hoped, industrial jobs; the fishery of Newfoundland may be sacrificed in part to the Bay D'Espoir Power project to provide electricity for the Electric Reduction Company, which ironically further dismembered that age-old industry for a time by pouring pollutants into Placentia Bay.

The Arrow valley in British Columbia was flooded by the Hugh Keenleyside Dam, one of the Columbia Treaty structures. Unlike most reservoirs in Canada, the valley was cleared of trees before the water began to rise, and it doesn't show the great mats of debris and stark grey spars customary in water projects. B.C. Hydro insists that all those people displaced received compensation that would enable them to live as well as before, and the public amenities such as highways were replaced to a standard much higher than that existing before flooding.

But Canadians have lost 40,000 acres of a magnificent valley, an area of small farms, white sand beaches, moderate climate and incredible beauty. How many such regions exist in Canada? Now the mountains slope steeply into the water, and the large new lake whips into five foot waves in minutes.

The Arrow Valley and its fiercely independent people were uniquely Canadian, and so were those whose lives were similarly changed by the Duncan Dam, and the Libby Dam. Hydro only cleared the Duncan Reservoir as far as visitors could see from the dam — around the first bend, it presents the same dead tangle of drowned trees found in most reservoirs in Canada. Libby displaces farmers and ranchers in one of the best parts of the Rocky Mountain Trench for human settlement. Their land will now be mud flats much of the year, as Libby backs the water 40 miles north across the border. Much winter wildlife range is also lost to the rising water.

The 150 mile long Mica Reservoir will be like a much larger Duncan; properly cleared it just might have been a fiord-like lake with arms leading deep into mountain valleys of incredible beauty — in fact, the area was removed from a

Provincial Park before its despoliation began. However, with a drawdown planned to be as much as 150 feet, it would probably have an ugly shoreline no matter how well it was cleared.

In Alberta, Louis Baudin supports his family on a fine farm that careful planning and hard work has created on the good soil of the McLeod River valley. The valley would be flooded by a dam under the PRIME scheme of things, or as envisioned by the Saskatchewan-Nelson Basin Study. It's difficult to see how a "fair market price" would compensate for the loss of his farm and those of his neighbours in this beautiful valley. "I don't know what I'll do. I guess just move to town and . . . kind of fit in with the rest. But my heart won't be in it." The land will be gone forever. The valley, which is the best farming land for perhaps 50 miles in any direction, forms the core of the larger social and economic unit of the region. With the valley and its people gone, the life of the community can be expected to disintegrate. There will not be enough people or tax revenue to maintain social centres, or the schools and their buses, or the local stores.

There is no evidence that southward diversions of the northward flowing rivers, or simply large scale development of them for hydro power, is compatible with the survival of the north as a land of biological integrity or as a land that will provide for a permanent population of native and white people. It is particularly noticeable that northern residents have not been considered in any way, as engineers proceed with plans for the removal of water from the rivers that nourish the north, and with other water developments. As Dr. Frank Quinn of the Department of the Environment has observed: "Northerners may have more to fear from the demands or indifference of their southern neighbours inside this country than from those who live outside. It will be imperative for the north to participate in Canadian water planning in the 1970's." Or as Dr. Ward Stevens of the Canadian Wildlife Service has warned northerners: "Be aware of what is proposed for your great wealth in water and aquatic resources. You have everything to lose. There is little evidence that your rights and your needs are being adequately considered in any of the published development plans I have seen."

One of the problems in northern water development is of course that there are so few people there to see what is going on, and even fewer with political weight. Not many Canadians have seen the great rivers and lakes and landscapes of the north, so they cannot appreciate what is being lost. Developments that might be unacceptable in the south proceed almost unnoticed in the north. In the north, we are often involved with "map-planning," where in some cases the top decision makers have not even bothered to see the land and water and people that they are manipulating. With only a few politically impotent people protesting; and with the developments supported by the weight of water or power agencies, construction interests, and the various groups that push development of any sort, the northern stage is set for destruction on an enormous scale. The worst of it will be done before the people of Canada are aware of what is being done. In fact, it is difficult to escape the notion that such programs as James Bay in Quebec and the Churchill-Nelson in Manitoba are being rushed ahead before reconsideration of the projects on ecological and social grounds is demanded by an aroused public.

In Quebec, much is being made of the fact that studies carried out during construction will provide information that will be of use in future such projects. Since no time has been allowed to collect the base-line data showing exactly what conditions exist prior to construction, such an argument is specious. Even if it were not, such knowledge as we already have is clearly not being applied and in fact is being completely ignored in the planning and decision making for our biggest water developments. And even if we were wise enough to use information collected now on projects in the future, our good intentions may not really matter much because the greatest damage will already have been done. Sadly, water development zeroes in on the best of our water resources, and as Dr. Robert Newbury of the University of Manitoba has pointed out, it is a mistake to consider our water resources equal in quality. They just happen to share the same colour on a map, and that can be misleading in terms of quality, for the finest of our natural water resources are being destroyed first.

Finally, let us once more turn to the past to examine a major water development that was highly visible and broadly approved by the people of Canada in spite of its high cost in social, environmental and financial terms. The St. Lawrence Seaway was the fruition of an economic and engineering dream that preceded actual construction by decades. Though Hydro authorities in Ontario took great pains to reduce social distress, 20,000 acres of Ontario alone were flooded, eliminating eight established communities and 225 farmers. There were 6500 people dislocated. The project hit the Caughnawaga Indian reserve near Montreal, and here, as in so many other communities, bitterness at the forced dislocation of people was the price of water development.

So the real cost of the St. Lawrence Seaway was very high. Yet in September of 1970, only eleven years after the Seaway was officially opened, Minister of Public Works Arthur Laing pronounced it obsolete. He declared it to be uneconomic and inefficient, due to changes in transportation technology. After a decade of operation the Seaway indebtedness had reached 400 million dollars, up from the 300 million dollar debt with which it had commenced operation. How can one now claim that "the public good" required that so much land be lost, so many communities disrupted and so many thousands of people uprooted? What is to be said to those who live in towns like Rossport, on the north shore of Lake Superior? Like many other Great Lakes fishing villages it has become largely a ghost town, its life blood having ebbed away with the disappearance of the lake trout. This fine fish was exterminated by the lamprey eel which seaway locks allowed to pass up the Great Lakes system along with the freighters. In just a few years, the commercial catch dropped from 5 million pounds annually to 400 pounds. The annual trout fishing derby at Rossport drew up to ten thousand people each July, injecting $300,000 into the local economy. Now the rotting docks of the town are silent all year round.

As our understanding of the nature of our water resources deepens, and as evidence of the true cost of manipulating them becomes irrefutable, a strange phenomenon is becoming evident. Even larger projects are being rushed ahead with no consideration whatever of social and environmental factors, except in a superficial way. The only evidence that any lessons whatever have been taken from the record, or that any recognition is given to rising public concern, is in the stepped up volume of public relations releases expressing the deep concern for "the ecology" on the part of whatever agency is involved.

It is a fact that governments and hydro and water authorities have carefully avoided assessment of the social and ecological effects of their massive water development projects. They have avoided studying the economics of their projects after construction is completed and all the bills are in. Such information is now accumulating gradually, but it is noticeable that it is not those responsible for authorizing or building the projects that are carrying out the studies. Typically, in fact, these agencies discount the validity of such evidence, and have done little to date to incorporate the results of research apart from the field of engineering, into their planning of new projects. This stands as a strange phenomenon indeeed when what is involved is the extremely rapid and permanent restructuring of vast areas of the world, and a complete disruption of some of our most important natural systems.

Our experience so far in water development has been with relatively simple projects, yet we have seen the unexpected repercussions from one-dam projects such as the Bennett Dam on the Peace River. It is evident that the scale on which we can expect complications to arise when dealing with a whole system of dams, diversions and canals as proposed in many regions of Canada would increase if only as a result of normal mathematical permutations and combinations. Additionally, however, through our complex strategies we are probably removing most of the natural resilience of a river system by which it can absorb some change and adjust to some level of abuse. We are proposing completely engineered systems, and we simply have no idea whether or not they will work, or for how long. We do know, however, that the present arrangement works very well, and can be expected to do so indefinitely. We might consider working with these natural systems rather than striving for the elimination of them.

Chapter 5

NAWAPA: dream or fact?

At a cost of one hundred billion dollars, the biggest public works program in history! Half a dozen dams about 1500 feet high, with the biggest more than 1700 feet, twice the height of any existing dam in the world! A reservoir in the Rocky Mountain Trench of British Columbia 500 miles long, 16 times larger in capacity than North America's largest manmade lake! A shipping canal crossing the prairies from the Great Lakes, perhaps even continuing to Vancouver, realizing at last the dream of a Northwest passage! Fifty different dams, canals, tunnels and reservoirs to move water from Northern Canada and Alaska to thirty three states of the United States, seven provinces of Canada, and three states of Mexico! It's called NAWAPA, the North American Water and Power Alliance, and it is an imaginative product from the drawing boards of the Ralph M. Parsons Company of Los Angeles, one of the world's largest engineering and construction firms.

Such a concept was perhaps inevitable after the 1963 decision of the United States Supreme Court allocating Colrado River water to Arizona in a way that would eventually reduce the amount of water California could take from that river. At any rate, in the spring of the following year, the Parsons firm launched its NAWAPA plan into a climate of opinion in the American Southwest that was ready to look at any way out of the dilemma posed by this decision. Southern California had always solved its water problems by reaching ever further for water to feed its growth, and here was a plan that made available to the arid Southwest enormous quantities of clear pure water from the north, since "vast amounts of water are pouring unused into northern seas and are irretreivably lost."

Or as the Parsons Company put it: "NAWAPA is a concept developed ... for collecting excess water of the Northwestern part of the North American continent and distributing it to the water deficient areas of Canada, the United States, and Mexico ... Water now wasting into the sea from Alaska, Canada and the Northwestern United States would be collected and stored in an interconnected system of reservoirs at relatively high elevations. By means of a reservoir-canal-river system the water would then be redistributed throughout the continent generating power as it descends to the sea. In addition, NAWAPA would, through its system of interconnecting rivers and canals, provide a network of navigable waterways throughout Canada and much of the United States."

The preparation and publication of the NAWAPA plan (at a cost of over a million dollars, according to Parsons) had immediate and far reaching effect. It was exuberantly praised by politicians and water resource officials in the American Southwest where the major benefits would accrue, and roundly condemned by many Canadians. U.S. Senator Frank Moss of Utah said: "This is a vast project, but we must not be deterred by its size. The challenges ahead are great and it will take just such a program to meet them." Canada's General A.G.L. McNaughton, however, termed NAWAPA, "a monstrous concept, not only in terms of physical magnitude, but also in another and more sinister sense, in that the promoters would displace Canadian sovereignty over the national waters of Canada, and substitute therefor a diabolic thesis that *all* waters of North America become a shared resource, of which most will be drawn off for the benefit of the midwest and southwest regions of the United States, where existing desert areas will be made to bloom at the expense of development in Canada."

There were Americans too who were appalled by the prospect of restructuring the face of the continent for what they considered to be unproven needs, and Daniel Luten of the University of California suggested: "If we must build NAWAPA, let us wait until we know our doom is at hand, and when our last realizable ambition is to amaze future archaeologists."

Amazed future generations certainly would be, for NAWAPA would drown many of the best intermountain valleys in British Columbia. Its central reservoir, a lake 500 miles long in the Rocky Mountain Trench of British Columbia, would inundate one of the nation's better living environments, a region of small farms, wildlife, and great beauty. The waves would roll over Cranbrook and Golden and Prince George and many smaller communities. The transcontinental highways and railroads would be cut. The

72   NAWAPA: dream or fact?

sale of Canadian water through NAWAPA or any other plan, means essentially the sale of great areas of the best of Canada's land as well.

NAWAPA might be described as the ultimate logical extension of the North American delight in bigness and our devotion to technology and growth. So it inevitably struck a responsive chord in water resource planners, dam building engineers, many politicians, and a wide assortment of dreamers. In considerable numbers they leaped to their drawing boards and before long a torrent of plans were published. For a few years, redesigning the water resources of the continent was very much in vogue, and maps of North America with penciled-in dams, diversions, canals, reservoirs and pumping stations were seriously discussed wherever water resource people met.

Lewis Gordy Smith, a retired U.S. Bureau of Reclamation engineer living in Denver, Colorado, vigorously promoted his "Western States Water Augmentation Concept" which would reverse the flow of the Liard River and part of the MacKenzie River using a series of dams and pumping stations. The water would be pushed up the Rocky Mountain Trench, passing through the Williston Reservoir behind Bennett dam on the Peace River, a dam which conveniently provides a plug on the Peace River that would otherwise have to be built. Then the northern water would be lifted into the Fraser River and shipped south to the United States. It would be routed either by way of the Fraser and a tunnel under the Cascade Mountains to the Columbia River, or by reversing both the Fraser and the Columbia down the Rocky Mountain Trench into the Kootenay River and on south into an elaborate distribution system serving the western United States.

NAWAPA and the Smith plan were schemes put forth by Americans for the diversion of Canadian water into the United States. But many other export schemes were conceived by Canadians. Professor Edward Kuiper, of the University of Manitoba, for instance, did some calculations that went even further than NAWAPA in designating Canadian water available for export and diversion. Of the 313 million acre feet flowing in the Nelson, Churchill, MacKenzie and Yukon Rivers, he considered it reasonable to divert 230 million acre feet, with probably more than 100 million acre feet of this actually available for export across the border. An example of how such figures are obtained can be seen in Professor Kuiper's analysis of the MacKenzie River.

"The average flow of the MacKenzie River at Fort Simpson is about 185,000,000 acre feet per year. The downstream riparian requirements in the future are difficult to foresee. There may be extensive oil drilling, there may be other mining developments in the valley, there is a possibility of limited agricultural development, there are some fishing interests in the delta regions. However, the sum total of all such requirements may not be equal to more than say 10,000,000 acre-feet per year. Hence, the flow available for diversion may be estimated in the order of 120,000,000 acre feet per year." Professor Kuiper can see no use at all being made of the Yukon river, where it is, and so suggests that its entire flow of 55,000,000 acre feet could be diverted.

Dr. E. Roy Tinney, another Canadian, put forth an alternative to NAWAPA in 1967 when he was a professor of engineering at Washington State University, and director of that state's Water Research Center. His Central North American Water Project, or CeNAWAP, would take water from the MacKenzie, Churchill, and Nelson Rivers in a diagonal direction from Great Bear Lake through Great Slave Lake, Lake Athabasca, to Lake Winnipeg. It would then branch south into the United States and east into Lake Superior. Tinney suggests his plan would provide 50 per cent more water for export at one third the cost of NAWAPA.

Dr. Tinney subsequently became employed in the Canadian Department of the Environment, Ottawa, where he is vitally involved in planning the use of Canada's water resources. His CeNAWAP plan has, it seems, become a source of embarrassment to him, and he apparently resents references that take it as a serious proposal. Many of those opposed to water export have suggested a sinister situation exists when one of the nation's foremost water authorities is himself the author of a gigantic water export scheme. And proponents of water export continually refer to the scheme, perhaps to enhance the "respectability" of the idea of export. The CeNAWAP plan appears in every list of export possibilities, and it seems particularly well thought of in such states as New Mexico, which would benefit particularly from this plan. Dr. Tinney states that his plan was put forth only to show that a much better scheme than NAWAPA could be devised if necessary, but that he does not personally advocate export of Canadian water to the United States.

Many other schemes were promoted in the 60's, such as

the "Magnum Canal" which would divert water from the Liard River across the prairies via the Peace, Athabasca, North and South Saskatchewan, Qu'Appelle and Souris Rivers into the Missouri. This plan, devised by Knut Magnusson of Alberta, would use a greatly flooded Lesser Slave Lake as a reservoir. A different approach was that of T.W. Kierans, a Sudbury engineer who would dam the rivers flowing into James Bay and reverse them, lifting the water southward over the divide so that it would flow into the Great Lakes. Kierans suggested it would then be used for regulating the levels of the lakes, and for export to water-short areas of the United States. McGill University Geographer Dr. Trevor Lloyd referred to NAWAPA in terms that apply to all such plans when he said: "Clearly we have here an exercise in sophomore civil engineering which has received far greater attention than it ever deserved. It underlines the danger, all too familiar to geographers, of allowing the drawing office to replace acquaintance with the land and the people as they really are. It is sometimes the path of wisdom to prevent the large-scale rearranging of nature, especially when it is based on inadequate knowledge, and hasty and ill-conceived plans."

Such schemes are innocent of even the most rudimentary consideration of the natural functioning of rivers and lakes, or of the animal and plant life that depends upon them. Nor do they recognise the fact that the nation that is Canada is the result of, and depends upon, the existing relationship between land and water, a thesis that will be developed in Chapter 10. No economic consideration of any degree of sophistication has been allowed to intrude, and the social disruptions inherent in the plans are never considered. The plans rest upon the assumptions that additional water is required in large volumes in the United States, and that great surpluses of water exist in Canada. We have seen that these are both highly questionable and dubious propositions.

When the NAWAPA plan appeared, it was the subject of a great deal of discussion. It was taken very seriously by Canadian parliamentarians and American politicians. Senator Frank Moss of the State of Utah was its most outspoken champion, and as Chairman of the U.S. Senate Special Subcommittee on Western Water Development, he was consistent and effective in advancing the cause of massive water development. The prestigious American publication *Science* editorialized: "The present NAWAPA concept is grand and imaginative. It is to be hoped that the Canadians will join us in this great project, but alternatives should be studied." As Dr. Frank Quinn of Canada's Department of the Environment has said, the import approach favours implementing in one massive sweep an ultimate solution to all foreseeable water problems. "One might well wonder whether a spirit of Manifest Destiny is not reborn [in the U.S.] in the continental use of Canadian waters."

But it soon became clear that Canada had nothing to gain and a nation to lose in the process of massive water export. General McNaughton led the opposition at first, engaging in the last great battle of his career which ended only with his death in 1966 at 79 years of age. In the succeeding years, the great cost of continental water schemes to Canada has become so obvious that few are actively promoting them in Canada. Even amongst dedicated water export enthusiasts it has become fashionable to deride NAWAPA particularly, and the great continental schemes generally. As Dr. Arleigh Laycock has said: "The proposal [NAWAPA] contains few advantages and many disadvantages for Canada, and the negative attitudes engendered have been widely applied to all export proposals." This is a matter for regret to Dr. Laycock, since as we have seen he has consistently promoted water export to the U.S. in a variety of ways.

Will NAWAPA or one of its cousins ever be built?

Roland P. Kelly is vice-president of the Ralph M. Parsons Company of Los Angeles, which designed NAWAPA. This personable engineer isn't at all downhearted about the criticism of the project. He is sure that NAWAPA, as a concept, will become a reality. It may not be called NAWAPA, and the dams and diversions may not be in precisely the locations suggested in the NAWAPA scheme, but he is convinced water movement in the spirit of NAWAPA will occur.

Why the optimism? Well, Mr. Kelly has been following with interest current water development projects on both sides of the border. "There are a number of construction projects now coming toward completion, namely Kettle Rapids in Manitoba, Mica Creek dam in British Columbia, which could become an integral part of it." So, without the overall plan, without any international treaties, and even though Canadians are a long way from any acceptance of the principal of water export, the Parsons company sees the pieces beginning to fall into place.

Fully to appreciate why things appear this way, it is necessary to review water development projects in existence, under construction, being planned or being studied in Canada from the west coast to Quebec. These include the Yukon-Taia project in the Yukon and British Columbia, the Bennett dam on the Peace River, the Columbia Treaty dams in B.C. and Montana, the Moran Dam on the Fraser and other water and power developments under discussion in that province, the PRIME program in Alberta, the Saskatchewan-Nelson Basin Study across the three prairie provinces and the completed Gardiner Dam on the South Saskatchewan River, and the Churchill-Nelson Hydro developments in Manitoba. Federal-provincial studies procede on northern Ontario Rivers flowing into James Bay to determine how the water could be used in their basins or diverted southward into Lake Superior, while five great rivers on the east side of James Bay are to be damned and diverted by the government of Quebec to generate power.

We will briefly examine what is involved in these plans and projects, then consider what their relationship might be to water export.

In Canada's North, the United States, Canada and British Columbia are together studying the Yukon-Taia project, which calls for five dams on the Yukon and Teslin Rivers. These would hold back the waters of the Yukon, Canada's fifth largest river, flooding several of the largest and most beautiful lakes of the North. Atlin Lake, Taku Lake, and Tagish Lake in British Columbia, along with Bennett Lake, Marsh Lake, and Lake Laberge, in the Yukon, all famed for their role in the Klondike Gold Rush, would be flooded. They would become little more than fluctuating reservoirs, and with them would die one of the greatest hopes for extensive tourism in the North.

The enormous quantities of power generated by Yukon-Taia would be expected to provide energy for mining and for the processing of ore. And a five hundred mile long high voltage transmission line would tie the plant into the west coast power system of which B.C. Hydro is a part. In recent years, however, it has become clear that the advantages once associated with the location of large power consumers such as aluminum smelters on tidewater near large hydro-electric power sources no longer exist. Resources economist Gunter Schramm has shown that it is more important for such industries to be closer to their markets, and that no more

Kitimats are likely. The large aluminum companies have indicated too that they are no longer interested in isolated locations just to acquire cheap power.

Yet water developments very seldom are related to any kind of realistic economic analysis. So the lack of economic justification for the Yukon-Taia project will certainly not be the deciding factor, particularly in a project with international implications. It would be quite in keeping with water development experience elsewhere for the proposal to acquire a life of its own, and to proceed even though the purpose for which the study was initiated no longer exists.

Many of Canada's largest water developments have been carried out in British Columbia. It is in this province that many of the nation's greatest rivers are to be found, and it is also in this province that development at any cost has been the governing credo. The "Two Rivers Policy" of B.C.'s former premier, W.A.C. Bennett, ended the free flow of two of the continent's greatest rivers, the Peace and the Columbia, with consequences of an economic, environmental, social and political nature that will be a lasting legacy. Bennett's government, through studies carried out by the B.C. Energy Board, was sorting out priorities as it considered the damming of most of the remaining rivers of the province when it was defeated August 30, 1972, by the New Democratic Party led by Premier Dave Barrett.

The damming of the Fraser River has been studied in detail, with engineers favouring a site at Moran Canyon, near Lillooet. Others being considered are the McGregory river, a northern tributary of the Fraser where great numbers of big spring salmon spawn; the Dean River, the greatest steelhead river on the coast; the Skeena, the Stikine and its tributary the Iskut; and the list goes on. All are very important salmon spawning-rivers. The NDP has long opposed Moran Dam, but its position with regard to all the other water development proposals in the B.C. Energy Board report is unknown as this book goes to press.

The Liard River is the largest tributary of the MacKenzie, which is itself second only to the Mississippi on the continent. British Columbia is studying several dam sites on the Liard for power generation, and presumably the federal government is doing the same on that section of the Liard flowing through the Yukon and Northwest Territories. Further south, in B.C., another flood control project proposed for the Fraser River system would place dams on the

Clearwater river within Wells Gray Park, flooding areas of great beauty with large wildlife and fish populations.

In Alberta, the PRIME program is a master plan for the use of the province's water. Its purpose is to divert to the south water presently flowing northward toward the Arctic ocean.

While no "need" has yet been specified, the first project of the PRIME scheme, the Big Horn Dam on the North Saskatchewan River, is underway and scheduled for completion in 1973. In addition to generating power, it will make possible the diversion of water from the North Saskatchewan River into the Red Deer River, for development of irrigation in east-central Alberta. Soil studies showed clearly that the soils of the area are not good for irrigation, and so the practicality of such a project is highly questionable. Yet the Big Horn proceeds and will create a lake 20 miles long, flooding the beautiful and historic Kootenay Plains area.

Big Horn is just the beginning of PRIME developments. Virtually all the magnificent free-flowing rivers spilling through mountain passes out onto the prairies would be manipulated in some way. The project which is receiving most attention at present is the Pembina Dam, about 60 miles west of Edmonton. It is of great significance. Diverting water out of the Pembina, a tributary of the Athabasca, into the North Saskatchewan River would be the first diversion of Arctic-flowing water into a more southerly stream. The implications of this will be explored in some depth later.

The PRIME plan has been officially shelved by the Conservative government which in 1971 defeated the Social Credit administration under whose authority the scheme had been developed. But it lives on as part of the federal-provincial Saskatchewan-Nelson Basin Study. This five million dollar study covering the three prairie provinces has as its objective, "a study of the water resources of the Saskatchewan-Nelson Basin, including the potential additional supply by diversion or storage. In carrying out the study, the Board will consider the engineering feasibility and cost of the many combinations of storage and-or diversion works needed to provide a firm water supply of varying amounts and varying seasonal distributions, at various selected points along the river system."

The eighteen "selected points" chosen by study engineers are not explained in the reports of the Saskatchewan-Nelson Basin Board. Presumably an arbitrary figure has been selected representing an amount of water that might be useful if at some time certain amounts of water were desired for irrigation or power developments or industrial expansion. Political sensitivities may be involved, but whatever the reasoning, there has been no public explanation of the need for these volumes of water at these points. Nor is there an explanation of the social goals of the prairie provinces that would require changing the entire water flow pattern of the region. There is no expressed recognition of the nature of the rivers as living systems whose manipulation will inevitably have enormous consequences upon the landscape of which they are a vital part. Yet studies continue on 54 dams and diversions, various combinations of which would convert the enormous Saskatchewan-Nelson basin into a gigantic plumbing system, the major purpose of which would be to move northward flowing water south.

Planners explain that the Saskatchewan-Nelson structures will be built only as required in a stage-by-stage, carefully-phased development. It is likely that this expresses correctly their intention, but experience in the United States where this sort of planning originates indicates that water development has a "stair-step" effect. One diversion has such great side effects, both predicted and unforeseen, that the only solution seems to be to divert water into the deprived river from still another watershed. As economist David Seckler of the University of California has put it with respect to the California experience: ". . . You go kind of in a domino fashion, stumbling further north, without end, really, and up to Canada probably."

One could expect such a sequence of events to occur if for example the Pembina dam were to be built as planned at Evansburg west of Edmonton, diverting water through the Sturgeon River into the North Saskatchewan. Inevitable damage to the Pembina basin downstream from the dam would require an infusion of water from the MacLeod River, which in turn would require as a technological bandaid water from the Athabasca River. Also, problems would have been building up downstream on the Athabasca, because both the Pembina and MacLeod are tributaries of it.

This sequence is all provided for in PRIME and in the Saskatchewan-Nelson study; what is not admitted is that the time over which the projects would be developed would likely be determined by the need to ameliorate the damage from each preceding division, rather than by any expressed need for water.

The Nelson River drains the watersheds of the Saskatchewan River from the West, the Red and Assiniboine from the south, and the Winnipeg from the east, into Hudson Bay. All the water from these hundreds of thousands of square miles of Canada meet in Lake Winnipeg. In one magnificent stream the Nelson carries it all, more than fifty million acre feet of water, to the sea. On the way it drops about 700 feet, and Manitoba Hydro plans to wring from the river all the energy that fall represents by means of a string of hydro plants along its length. The first major dam at Kettle Rapids has been completed, and others are expected to follow in fairly rapid succession. To provide even more water to spin the generators in these plants, it is intended to dam the Churchill River, about one hundred miles further north, and divert its flow of some twenty million acre feet across country into the Nelson. The environmental and social implications of this rearrangement of major northern rivers are enormous, as we discussed in Chapter 4.

In 1965, the federal government and the government of Ontario agreed to study the possible diversion southward of waters normally flowing into James Bay and Hudson Bay. And so a Co-ordinating Committee on Northern Ontario Water Resources studies spent several years on studies "to determine present and future requirements for such waters, and to assess alternative possibilities for the utilization of such waters locally or elsewhere through diversions." Though federal officials have indicated the water would be used at the site, presumably for power, Ontario Hydro has indicated that it is not particularly interested in developing these northern rivers for hydro-electric power. Maps associated with the reports of the study committee show clearly that the studies provide for the movement of large volumes of water south to Lake Superior.

Federal officials state that any diversion into the Great Lakes would be for the purpose of stabilizing their levels. The Great Lakes cover an area of 95,000 square miles, and their vast storage capacity makes them one of the best naturally-regulated water systems in the world. But of course, some fluctuations are inevitable. When the water drops, as it did in 1964, navigation interests proclaim that something must be done about it. When it rises to higher than normal levels as it did in 1952, people with property along the shore may be disturbed. Some suggest that control structures between the lakes might even out the fluctuations somewhat, but even this is extremely difficult because of the sheer size of the lakes. The very factor that under natural conditions maintains the lakes at such remarkably stable levels, makes it extremely difficult for man to control the lake levels according to his own wishes.

When consideration is given to diverting southward water that normally flows into James Bay to help stabilize the lakes, the problems encountered appear insoluble. As M.W. Thompson, engineering advisor to the International Joint Commission has pointed out, one cannot consider diversions either into or out of the Great Lakes unless rain and snowfall, and rates of evaporation can be predicted at least two or three years in advance. Otherwise, water added into Lake Superior at a time of low levels could be flooding lower lakes two or three years later when average or above average precipitation had brought those Lakes to normal levels. As an example of the delayed response in lower lakes to changes in water levels in upper lakes, three and a half years after a change in the water supply in Lake Huron has occurred, only 60 per cent of it will have yet been felt in the outflow from Lake Ontario. Diversion of Northern Ontario rivers in order to stablize the Great Lakes seems an untenable proposal.

In Quebec, an enormous hydro power development involving dams and diversions on five large rivers flowing into James Bay has been announced. As is normal in Canadian water development, little information is available about the plans, but estimates of cost range up to ten billion dollars, and about a quarter of the land mass of the province is in the watersheds to be affected. Six to seven thousand Indians will have their largely traditional way of life disrupted. Consequences of the project were discussed in Chapter 4. The decision was reached in private by Premier Bourassa of Quebec on the basis of two reports by consulting engineering firms which made no comments whatever on the possibility of environmental or social disruptions. The project is generally considered in Quebec to be a social, environmental, economic and political gamble of enormous proportions.

With this brief look at major water development programs across most of the nation, we can now come back to our original question. Will NAWAPA, or one of the other continental water diversion plans ever be built? Let's beg the question once more until we see what relationship the all-Canadian developments we've outlined might have to larger water export schemes.

The Yukon-Taia project in the Northwest would begin the reversal of flow of northern rivers that is the essence of NAWAPA or any other export plan. More dams further north in Alaska and the Yukon could add still more northern water to the southward flow. Dams built for power generation on such rivers as the Stikine and the Skeena would serve to keep the southward flow of water from moving out to the Pacific through the mountain passes, and would also generate power to spin the pumps that would have to lift the great new river upwards toward the 500 mile long reservoir in the Rocky Mountain Trench.

Power dams strung out along a river with the toe of one dam at the head of the reservoir of the next one, need only a simple change in machinery to reverse their function — with power fed into them, and the turbines reversed to serve as pumps instead of as generators, the flow of the river can be reversed. If Hydro dams are built at the sites being studied by B.C. Hydro on the Liard River, this great river which contributes 60 million acre feet to the MacKenzie each year could be reversed and made to flow down the Dease River and eventually into the Rocky Mountain Trench in accordance with a NAWAPA scheme. Or the water could be backed directly up the trench via the Kechika River valley as in the "Smith" plan. Smith would add to the reversed flow of the Liard by diverting MacKenzie River water into its own tributary, the Liard, at Fort Simpson.

Once in the Rocky Mountain Trench, the water would pass through the Williston Reservoir on the Peace River. The Bennett Dam has conveniently plugged the only opening to the east out of the trench. There are three breaks in the west wall of the trench further south; the Fraser, Columbia, and Kootenay Rivers. The Columbia will be sealed off by the Mica Dam, presently under construction, and the Kootenay River is now plugged by the Libby Dam in Montana which even now floods 40 miles back into Canada. That leaves only the Fraser, and the highly controversial Moran Dam near Lillooet would be the beginning of a solution to that problem. Fraser River development plans apparently require that another dam to be built upstream of Quesnel, and that will provide the final stopper in the walls of the Rocky Mountain Trench. With some channelling and pumping, great volumes of Canadian water can then be moved to the United States.

The situation in the prairie provinces is even more clear. The PRIME program and the Saskatchewan-Nelson Basin Study are specifically designed to show how northern water can be moved south. If some of these projects are followed through, large volumes of water will be flowing near the international border, and it will take little more than a figurative "turning of the tap" to transfer water across the border, probably into the Missouri River system via the Milk River in Alberta, or via the Souris River in Saskatchewan or Manitoba. So it can be seen that the studies currently being carried out by the federal government and the prairie provinces will provide guidance for the construction of water projects that would fulfill most of the requirements of water export. Lake Diefenbaker, the reservoir behind the Gardiner Dam on the South Saskatchewan River, is the key to stabilizing flows throughout much of such a system, and it of course has already been built.

In northern Manitoba, completion of the Churchill-Nelson hydro scheme currently under construction by Manitoba Hydro will harness a flow of about 70 million acre feet toward Hudson Bay through a series of hydro plants stepped one above the other on the Nelson River. It would be quite possible to use the same structures to reverse the flow of the river, and draw the water off from the southern tip of Lake Winnipeg and Lake Manitoba for diversion to the United States through the Missouri River system or eastward to the Great Lakes. This would fit into such schemes as Dr. Roy Tinney's CeNAWAP, and others as well.

The sort of reasoning that might bring about such a shift in the use of hydro facilities on the Nelson River is provided by Professor E. Kuiper of the University of Manitoba. "One acre-foot of water, situated in Lake Winnipeg and descending through the eight projected power plants on the Nelson River with a total head of about 600 feet, would produce an amount of electric energy worth about one dollar. Therefore, if this same acre-foot could be exported at a $20 profit, we would naturally produce the required electrical energy by other means (coal or nuclear) and sell the water."

The federal-provincial studies in Northern Ontario clearly show ways of diverting water destined for James Bay and Hudson Bay southward into the Great Lakes. Water export enthusiasts on both sides of the border often suggest that this would be the manner by which water export would first take place. Some of the proposals for making use of greater volumes of water in the Mississippi system and throughout the Great Lakes states were outlined in Chapter 2. Citizens in Northern Ontario have become greatly alarmed about such a possibility, because while government authorities continually try to be reassuring, studies continue that would make implementation of export plans possible in a relatively short time. Suspicions were heightened in January of 1970 when the Ontario government admitted involvement of the United States Army Corps of Engineers in studies of ice and water flow conditions in Northern Ontario. Ecological and archaeological studies are proceeding in areas that would be flooded if dams and diversions were to proceed as outlined in maps prepared by the federal-provincial Co-ordinating Committee on Northern Ontario Water Resources Studies.

The enormous James Bay Hydro project planned by the Government of Quebec is possible only because of the interest of American power interests in the electricity it would generate. But with respect to the export of water, the comments of Dr. J. A. Spence of McGill University, Montreal in April of 1972 are of interest. After describing some of the enormous ecological and social impacts that could be expected in the James Bay project area, Dr. Spence said: "I would like finally to raise one skeleton from the closet — if the original North American Water and Power Alliance [NAWAPA] plans proposed several years ago are recalled, it will be remembered that the eastern part of this fantastic scheme involved diversion of "excess" water flowing into James, Hudson and Ungava Bays to the south to dilute out the polluted rivers of the U.S.A. It was to start where the James Bay development is planned to end, at a proposed reservoir — the Kaniapiskau Reservoir in Central Ungava. The present proposals of the James Bay Development Corporation would be a useful start towards such a Water and Power Alliance, and towards ruining our northlands and throwing away our natural resources."

Back, finally, to our question. Will NAWAPA, or one of the similar schemes for the export of water to the United States ever be built?

It is extremely unlikely that any huge engineering scheme called NAWAPA or appearing to be similar to it will ever be initiated. After several years of often highly emotional discussion, no politician could sell to the Canadian people a name that has come to mean "sell-out". Some Canadians see in the various water developments built, underway, proposed or under study evidence of a master plan that will only be admitted when it is well past the point of no return. But the number of people that would be involved in such a plan would be so large that keeping it under cover would be impossible. Not even cabinet ministers have much luck in keeping important secrets in Ottawa. So it seems unlikely that those opposed to continental water development will ever be confronted by a proposal that they can openly contend with. In fact, opposition to such programs will probably always be met by a political response that is in complete agreement with those opposing water export.

What is much more likely is that water development will proceed in Canada along the same lines as in the past, and in accordance with plans and studies currently under way. Much of the development will be for hydro-electric power, of which considerable amounts will be sold in the United States. This is the case in the James Bay program of Quebec, and also in the Nelson River program in Manitoba. It has been shown how a great many of Canada's hydro developments can be readily adapted to the export of large quantities of water, and that in fact they involve dams in almost precisely the locations called for in continental diversion schemes. Again, this is not necessarily because of some great overall plan, but because there are certain logical places on any river to put dams from an engineering viewpoint. It doesn't matter much what the reasons may be for putting the dams in place — the fact is that they will be correctly sited for water export, as well as for their stated purpose.

The situation with respect to actual diversion proposals is more straightforward. In the case of Northern Ontario, water would be moved into the Great Lakes from where it could readily be drawn off to the south. In fact, diverted water would probably have to be taken out of the lakes, because evidence is growing that any attempt to bring in water to control the level of the Great Lakes could be disastrous.

On the prairies, Alberta's PRIME program and the broader Saskatchewan-Nelson Basin Study have as their stated aim the movement of northern water to the southern regions of the country, or the investigation of such a possibility. This is of course precisely what is required for export, and in fact some Canadians, notably Dr. Arleigh Laycock, recommend that these projects be made larger than Canadian "needs" would require so that water can be exported using these structures. He suggested there would be economies of scale realized, and American money would be available for construction.

Let us create a scenario, then, of what might happen as Canadian water development proceeds on its present course. Experience around the world and throughout North America shows clearly that the economic aspects of massive water development are always grossly miscalculated, with costs underestimated and benefits overstated. It is likely that continued water development will therefore mean a great increase in the enormous indebtedness already incurred for water development in Canada.

Then, of course, we will find as we become involved in these ever larger and more complex developments that the environmental impact of them will be enormous. This is certainly turning out to be the case with many single dam projects; the permutations and combinations of effects that whole systems of dams and diversion may have is almost totally unkown.

We are, then, moving toward a situation in which we will have great, uneconomic water developments across the country, creating ecological havoc of all kinds. They will have brought large volumes of water close to the border in all-Canadian projects, and most of the structures required to facilitate diverting still larger quantities south will have been built for hydro purposes. The temptation to recoup some of these enormous costs by turning the water across the border will be very great. The real cost of bringing the water down to the border would not be economic for the Americans, but of course they wouldn't have to pay it all since Canada would have already absorbed most of the costs in what were to be domestic projects. Canadian governments would probably be ready to negotiate what would be in effect stop-loss prices to get out from under the worst of the burden of debt, and to make up in a small way for the environmental destruction that would clearly be evident and irrevocable.

We could add a few more elements to the scenario. Suppose at last a breakthrough in technology makes fusion or solar power available in quantity, as can be expected within this century. Power would be available to run the turbines within hydro dams as pumps rather than as generators, thereby reversing whole rivers as described earlier. Other trends in Canada at present indicate that when the time for such decisions arrives, even more of the Canadian economy will have become dominated by the multi-national corporations of the United States. We will be faced by the harsh reality that ever-greater continentalism has, in the words quoted earlier from historian Donald Creighton, "divorced Canadians from their history, crippled their creative capacity, and left them without the power to fashion a future for themselves." Such economic integration will enable the Americans to exert enormous political pressure on a Canada that will have gone very far in preparing the dams and diversions required for the export of water.

This sort of scenario, with perhaps more or fewer acts and performers, will likely lead Canadians into selling the only resource that they still largely control. It is a scenario which appears inevitable if present trends in Canada are followed. It shows too that Canadian politicians will, in all honesty, deny any intention of exporting water until just before it actually occurs. They will at that time be as appalled as the people of Canada at the lack of choice the nation has with respect to its water resources.

It is clear that the great danger lies not in the grandiose water export schemes such as NAWAPA that have been so thoroughly criticized in Canada. The real threat to Canada's water resources, and perhaps to the nation's existence, lies in the hydro-electric and water diversion projects within Canada that are at this moment under construction, or are being planned and studied.

Chapter 6
The economics of water development

The enormous cost of water development in social and environmental terms is becoming very clear. It would be reasonable to assume, then, that such projects must have overwhelming economic advantages. An examination of the economics of water development is the intended purpose of this chapter — but the reader with even a modest understanding of modern economic thought must expect to feel something like Alice in Wonderland as he tries to find logical economic procedures underlying many of our great water projects of both past and future.

One of the difficulties in dealing with such a subject is the scarcity of information about either completed or planned projects. It is uncommon for public assessment of any kind to be carried out after water projects have been completed. Gilbert F. White of the University of Colorado is one of the world's leading authorities in the field, and he has stated: "We could fill a large room with documents drawing up what are considered the best plans for and analyses of problems in river basins around the world. On the other hand, the literature about what has happened after any of the projects have been carried out can be assembled on one end of a small table. For example, no evaluation of the Tennessee Valley Authority has been undertaken. We have no satisfactory explanation of why, thirty years after the TVA was started in order to develop the economy of the region, the major part of the Tennessee Valley is still considered an underprivileged area of Appalachia, deserving special subsidy contributions from the federal government for further improvement." TVA has long been considered, of course, as a model of comprehensive river basin development.

Probably the only detailed economic analysis of major river development in Canada was that carried out by American economist John Krutilla on the economic implications of the Columbia River Treaty. Another study was carried out on major developments further downstream on the Columbia by George Macinko in 1963. An extremely useful book on the economics of large interbasin transfers of water by Charles W. Howe and K. Williams Easter was published in 1971. There are of course occasional papers on various projects, but for the most part any assessment of what has been done must be interpreted from limited data, and through examination of the methods used to justify water developments. First, then, we will look at some completed projects for which information and opinion is available, then we will examine how the economic aspects of the original decisions were made and continue to be carried out for future projects. Finally, we shall discuss some of the economic principles that, on the basis of the most recent work in this field, should be considered in assessing future projects.

The Columbia River Treaty, signed by Prime Minister John Diefenbaker for his Conservative government in 1961, and ratified by the Liberals under Prime Minister Lester Pearson in 1964, was preceded by twenty years of wrangling and bitterness. That atmosphere still prevails whenever the topic is discussed. The treaty provided for three dams to be built in Canada and for a dam in the United States on the Kootenay River that would back water north across the border 40 miles into the Rocky Mountain Trench of British Columbia. The environmental and social effects of the Arrow, Duncan, and Mica dams in Canada, and the Libby Dam in Montana were discussed in chapter 4. Our primary interest here is in the economics of the Treaty.

Dr. W.R. Derrick Sewell of the University of Victoria in 1966 assessed some of the lessons and implications of the Treaty, particularly as they might be applied in other river basins. He summarized: "The Columbia River experience . . . emphasizes that economic considerations tend to play a subordinate role in the final decision-making. The importance of taking such considerations into account is generally recognized by those in charge of the planning but various factors inhibit the necessary evaluations — past decisions, prior committments to particular projects, the engineer's scepticism of the value of economic studies, the lack of analytical tools, and the lack of trained personnel to carry out the studies. The general result is that economic studies occupy a rather minor place in over-all investigations, and are often delayed until most of the decisions have been made, or are not undertaken at all. Millions of dollars were spent on engineering studies, most of them using basically the same information; yet only a few thousand dollars were spent on economic studies, though investments of several hundred million dollars were being contemplated."

The purpose of the Treaty was quite simple — to store fifteen and a half million acre feet in Canada to be released in such a way as to maximize power generation downstream in the American power plants which dominate almost the entire length of the U.S. section of the river. It was to provide flood protection for U.S. communities as well. The water stored in this manner is essentially new water for the Americans, since prior to the construction of Treaty dams it had to be spilled over the dams during seasonal high flows. It therefore was not available at times of low flows when more power could be generated if sufficient water could be passed through the turbines. Under the terms of the treaty, the Americans simply state how much water they want to cross the border at any particular time, and Canada must comply. In other words, the United States now controls the entire Columbia River, including the two hundred and seventy miles of it that lie within Canada, draining almost 40,000 square miles of British Columbia. The Columbia, Duncan, and Kootenay Rivers, on which are located the four Treaty dams, are the central features of the largest and best sections of southeastern British Columbia.

Specific criticism of the economics of the treaty was evident throughout the negotiations and in the years following. General A.G.L. McNaughton as Chairman of the Canadian Section of the Internation Joint Commission fought desperately to prevent what he termed a sell-out of Canadian resources. For the fact is that Canada was paid nothing at all for this water which now was available for use not only for the generation of power, but for agricultural, industrial and municipal uses in the United States. General McNaughton estimated in 1966 that these benefits should have been worth $2.65 billion dollars over the first 30 years of the treaty. Larratt Higgins of Toronto is one of Canada's leading energy resource economists, and he spoke vigorously against the treaty on economic grounds. In 1966, he suggested that the value of the water stored behind the Treaty dams in Canada, using the American's own evaluation of forty dollars per acre foot, amounted to $620 million per year in the United States.

Such figures are in startling contrast to those negotiated in the Columbia Treaty. Canada received a single payment of

$273.3 million for the benefits the U.S. gained by being able to generate more power downstream. The U.S. also paid $68.3 million for flood control benefits derived in the U.S. from the dams. Another $112 million accrued in interest and other payments in the years following the signing of the treaty. This money was supposed to pay for the dams, and also for half the generators to be installed in Mica dam, the only one of the th ee Canadian dams that would have its own power generating facilities.

During negotiations and afterwards, Higgins, McNaughton and others insisted that there was ro way in which these amounts would pay for the facilities required under the Treaty in Canada. As Larratt Higgins has put it: "It will cost Canada about 100 million to give the Columbia away," and subsequent events have proven that his estimates were conservative. Canadian taxpayers, it has become clear, will be paying close to $200 million dollars for the privilege of turning control of the continent's fourth largest river over to the United States. In addition, Canada has donated to the U.S. at no cost at all some of British Columbia's finest valleys and has disrupted the lives of thousands of its citizens. And even this in no way includes the potential value these valleys had in terms of increased settlement; or for recreation and forest and mineral resource exploitation.

The Columbia River Treaty — The Economics of an International River Basin Development by John V. Krutilla provides the only exhaustive economic study we have of water development in Canada. Dr. Krutilla's conclusions are startling. After Premier Bennett decided to go ahead with the Peace River power project, attractive possibilities existed for managing the Columbia and Peace jointly as part of the north-south intertie that existed between B.C. and the Pacific Northwest States. In such a situation, the Hugh Keenleyside Dam which flooded the Arrow Valley, and either the Libby Dam or the Duncan Dam, were not required to fulfill the economic purposes of the treaty. In other words, even accepting the presumptions of the treaty and the political ramifications of it, only two dams were needed to obtain the economic benefits it was designed to produce. For reasons we will explore in the next chapter, four dams were built anyway. Dr. Krutilla points out: "In this international undertaking the opportunities for realizing significant economies through pooling technical possibilities were, on the whole, missed."

The tragedy of the Columbia River Treaty is now clear, and its cost in economic, social, and environmental terms is evident. Yet somehow, to many in positions of power the lesson does not seem to be clear. It is understandable that those who were involved in the Treaty will have positions to defend, but in June 1970, Vancouver mining promoter Jack Austin said: "We hope that the practice of resource sharing as explained in the Columbia River Treaty is an indication of the tendency of the same parties [U.S. and Canada] to deal with other resource problems in the same way." Shortly after, he was appointed federal deputy minister of Mines, Energy and Resources, thereby becoming a key person in designing Canada's energy relationships with the United States. Sadly enough, Canada's resource policies do indeed appear to be following the model of the Columbia River Treaty, often with similar economic results.

Faulty though they may have been, at least there were some figures put against the costs and benefits of the Columbia Treaty dams. In Saskatchewan, $182 million was committed to the building of what was to be the Gardiner Dam on the South Saskatchewan River with no such crass considerations. The Dam was an act of faith — it simply had to be a good thing to capture the waters of the South Saskatchewan as it flowed by the dry prairie fields. Spread across them, the water would bring great prosperity, and newspaper articles of the nineteen fifties spoke of a great city rising by the river, with industry processing the produce of irrigated farms, powered by the electricity that would be produced at the Dam. Federal officials spoke confidently of irrigating 500,000 acres, and of farmers who no longer would spend the hot summers anxiously searching the sky for rainclouds. For such a dream, it was unseemly to demand stringent cost-benefit analyses — the question was not an economic one, but rather a question of financing: could enough money be parted from federal and provincial government treasuries to build the Dam? It could, and it was — in July, 1958, Prime Minister John Diefenbaker and Saskatchewan Premier T.C. Douglas signed an agreement to share the costs of building the South Saskatchewan River Dam. Canada would pay 75% of the cost, and Saskatchewan 25%, with its share not to exceed $25 million. There had been plenty of opposition to it, including a Royal Commission that reported adversely. But if the Dam was on shaky ground economically, it was built on a rock as far as practical politics was concerned — and that has been the key to water development across the continent, and indeed around the world.

As the years went by after construction began in 1959, and as the big machines piled up the earth in a ribbon more than 16,000 feet long spanning the valley of the South Saskatchewan, doubts too were rising. Soil surveys showed that only 200,000 acres were irrigable, rather than the 500,000 that were projected when the project was approved. Many in Saskatchewan don't ever expect to see even that much land watered. It turned out that the dryland farmers of that part of Saskatchewan were quite satisfied with their way of life and wanted no part of the totally different sort of farming required in irrigation agriculture. These farmers confronted provincial leaders with their demands to be left alone or be adequately compensated. Farm leaders, the farm newspapers and university experts were among those who saw no benefits accruing to farmers, no markets for the high value crops that were being promoted for the area, and no hope of pacifying those farmers who wanted to stay with their dryland farming methods.

Markets for the products of irrigated land are a particularly delicate problem. Farm products in general are characterized by what is called an "inelastic" demand — that is, it takes a considerable price reduction to move more of a particular food product. Suppose, for example, the quantity of carrots being produced at a given time are being sold at a price that provides the grower with a reasonable return for his labour and investment. A relatively small additional quantity of carrots will create a surplus of that product, and it will take a rather drastic drop in the price of all carrots for more to be sold than formerly. Consumer preference and rate of consumption of carrots or almost any other farm product is quite fixed, in part by the "inelasticity of the human stomach," and only a very remarkable price change will cause the consumer to buy more. As a general rule, then, increased agricultural production exerts a strong downward pressure on prices.

And so any suggestion of adding irrigated land, which must produce these high value crops to make any economic sense, should be looked at in the context of the market for these products. Each irrigated acre produces very large quantities of vegetables and has a vastly greater effect on that market than would an additional acre of a low value crop such as grain which can be grown on dry land. Even if promotion and subsidies of various kinds can persuade processors of farm products to locate near new irrigation districts, the impact may be felt in established markets far away. For instance, Alberta potatoes may compete with those from Prince Edward Island for a place on the tables of Ontario. Charles Howe and William Easter have documented this in the American experience. "The expansion of irrigated acreage displaces, through the market, production in other areas. When this irrigated acreage is made profitable only under continuing federal or state subsidies, it clearly is economically inefficient."

It can have enormous social ramifications as well. Howe and Easter show that the expansion of irrigation in the United States during the twenty years following World War II, always in programs heavily subsidized by the taxpayer, displaced between five and seven million acres of farm land in non-reclamation areas, particularly in the South. This in turn resulted in unemployment for large numbers of farm workers in those areas, and many of them migrated to the cities of the north, where they contributed to urban social problems as well as to their own unhappiness. Income losses in the areas forced out of production ranged from $50 million to $170 million.

Similar difficulties are expected in California as the new State Water Project brings large new acreages into production. As it happens, the federal government in the United States is looking critically at the huge subsidies being paid to large cotton growers. This was expected to be an important crop in the newly irrigated areas, but if subsidies for large growers are removed, or reduced, University of California agricultural economist Dr. David Seckler sees real difficulties ahead. "They are going to have to go into fruit, nuts, vegetables, which have a very limited market, so that this tremendous increase in acreage (brought about by the State Water Project) in the limited market is going to cause massive reductions in prices, hurting established agriculture as well as the state." It is a mind-boggling fact, then, that in California the only way subsidized water will pay off for irrigation is if heavily subsidized crops are grown. Similarly, we saw in Chapter I how the importation of water into central Arizona (a major factor in the growing demand for Canadian water exports) would result in higher water prices for the farmers and other users in that state. Remember Alice in Wonderland?

The implications of all this for the South Saskatchewan project are clear. Tom Melville-Ness, publisher of the Saskatchewan Wheat Pool's newspaper *The Western Producer*, said back in 1963: "There's no certainty of high cash crops and no market for them. The truck gardeners of Manitoba take care of the whole needs of the Prairies and still have 35% of their crops for export." He went on to state: "It's unfair to charge the cost of the dam to agriculture. The farmers won't benefit. They can only expect one good crop every five years as a result of irrigation. It's been proven that three out of five irrigation farmers go broke." The new irrigation farmers of Saskatchewan would also have to compete with the well-established irrigation areas of Alberta, who have had the advantages of much less costly structures long since written off, a more favorable climate, and established markets.

If the time comes when more agricultural produce is needed, there are many ways in which this can be effected much more economically than by large irrigation projects with their massive public investments. Increased efficiency of existing irrigation systems is certainly one of these; and small supplementary systems for use in regions normally supplied with adequate rainfall can be developed as required at a fraction of the cost of the large dryland projects. The use of modern farm management techniques, better varieties, fertilizers, and the whole arsenal of better practises known to modern agriculture can be brought into more extensive use as required.

The economic details are not readily available, but it appears that by 1971, about 13,000 acres were being irrigated in the South Saskatchewan project. No studies have been published to show what the people of Canada have paid per acre for this land to be brought under irrigation. Certainly such calculations would be illuminating, as was John Krutilla's study of the Columbia Treaty. The amount of subsidy involved in the associated works that brought water to the potash mines of the province is similarly unknown, and no figures allocating the costs of the dam between irrigation, industry, and electrical power generation are available for analysis.

In trying to find similar situations for comparative purposes, one possible indication of the kinds of costs involved in switching from dryland grain farming to irrigation farming might be found in the Columbia Basin Project in the

State of Washington. Begun in the 1930's with the construction of Grand Coulee Dam, about one million acres were to be irrigated. But dry land farmers withdrew about 300,000 acres of that, preferring to continue growing wheat. That was much of the best land in the project. The project actually began operation in 1948, and in 1963 geographer Dr. George Macinko reported: "Little more than a decade has elapsed since water was first brought to project lands, and already serious difficulties have been encountered. Development is virtually at a standstill, with less than half of the planned acreage under cultivation; and future growth is uncertain." In 1970, the Bureau of Reclamation, the agency responsible for the project, reported that it had cost $1,098 per acre to bring water to the land, of which the farmers were expected to pay $132 over time. The remainder, it was expected, would be paid off by power revenues from the power plant in the dam.

As an aside, it is interesting to note that in 1964, with the Columbia River Treaty an accomplished fact, the U.S. Bureau of Reclamation was looking forward to a considerable expansion of irrigated acreage, not only because of the extra water made available through regulation of the Columbia in Canada, but because the large additional quantities of power that could now be generated would pay for more irrigation projects. One might also suggest that the farm products grown under the subsidization made possible by storage dams in Canada would be competing with the farm products of Canada, and particularly those of the Okanagan and Fraser valleys. Another uncharged cost to Canadians of the Columbia Treaty.

Even the mind-boggling costs of irrigation in Washington drastically understate the economic disadvantages of the project, because under the rules by which the Bureau of Reclamation operates, projects have fifty years to be paid for, and no interest is charged on that amount! Since interest rates are so important a factor that a shift of one per cent can make the difference between feasibility or impossibility in huge hydro projects, it can be seen that the "no interest" provision amounts to yet another enormous subsidy.

The American figures are useful in two respects; they serve to indicate the sort of economics involved in large irrigation projects, and they show also the kind of use to which Canadian water would be put, if it were exported south of the border.

As the apparent irrigation benefits of the dam on the South Saskatchewan diminished, the potential for recreation of the new lake with almost 500 miles of shoreline received increasing emphasis. In June 1963 the *Financial Post* headed a story on the dam: "This could become the world's most costly swimming pool." It is not yet clear how important the reservoir will be for this purpose, but many trees have been planted, some beaches built and parks created. In some places, however, the shoreline continues to slump into the reservoir as erosion occurs, in some places creating high clay cliffs and in others wide shallows and mud flats, both factors that will have a limiting effect on recreational use. Time will show how great a recreational attraction a reservoir like this will be, for in addition to its physical disadvantages it is a considerable distance from centres of population. But one point can be seen clearly—the people of Canada will have paid handsomely for each day of recreation that their fellow citizens and visitors enjoy on Lake Diefenbaker.

The usual response to critical economic analysis of water projects is that while the project itself may not make economic sense, the people of the region and the nation as a whole will benefit because of the growth and development that will take place, first through the construction activity itself, and then through the permanent development that will accrue from a bountiful supply of water or of energy, in the case of hydro dams. This is a view that is widely subscribed to by lobbies which promote water development in the general belief that any water development has to be good, or by Chambers of Commerce who see their area benefitting from such development. Such a view is also pushed by the individuals and groups who stand to benefit through increased land values, construction contracts, and other such factors.

In a dry area, it is admittedly difficult to avoid feeling that plentiful water would be of tremendous benefit. To make the desert "bloom like a rose" has long been considered an admirable cause, and on the dry short-grass plains of southeastern Saskatchewan it is easy to believe that with plentiful water prosperity is inevitable. Yet there is little evidence to support this. There are a great number of regions with bountiful supplies of water that certainly have not become centres of growth. And if water is brought in to an area, or a river like the Saskatchewan is developed at great cost, what sort of industries can be induced to move in? The authoritative text *Water Supply* answers that question this way: "If water is scarce in an area and this constitutes a barrier to development, subsidizing the water will attract precisely the wrong kind of industries in view of the real natural advantages and disadvantages of the region." In other words, uneconomic water developments promoted for the supposed advantage of economic growth to the area will quite likely harm the region it is supposed to be subsidizing, in addition to siphoning off funds that could be better used for other purposes.

Resource economist Dr. James Crutchfield states: "It is no more unnatural that water be scarce and expensive in some areas, and abundant and cheap in others, than it is to find regional differences in the supply and price of land, transportation facilities or other natural and man-made economic factors. The urge to move vast amounts of water over vast distances ignores the distinct possibility that it would be cheaper and more effective for water-short regions to specialize in economic activities that require little water." The situation is the same whether the subsidization of water results from moving water long distances, as suggested by Dr. Crutchfield, or in large-scale development within a particular river basin.

A fairly typical argument by those promoting water diversions is that of Arleigh Laycock of the University of Alberta. He suggests: "In Canada well over half the population lives within 100 miles of the Southern border. Water can be brought to centers in these areas fairly cheaply if needed." We will be looking at the key aspects of such statements in this chapter — the question of "need", and of just *how* "cheaply" must be closely examined. But the issue to be considered here is that of the logic of moving water to an area where shortages are claimed to exist.

Crutchfield suggests that such water movement, "flies in the face of common sense as well as long-accepted economic analysis, both of which suggest, as a possible alternative, the inter-regional movement of goods rather than productive inputs. The fact that arable agricultural land, urban land, minerals, and forests must be used where they are does not deny them to those in other regions. Economic production in each region will simply be tailored to the level and composition of the factor equipment with which it is endowed, and the resulting regional 'surpluses' exchanged. Trade is an excellent offset to the immobility of the basic resources tied to particular bits of land. Water is obviously more mobile than land or forests, but only in degree. The crucial question is the cost of moving water relative to the economic cost of making the next best adjustment; and since the cost of moving large quantities of water is very high indeed, there are good a priori reasons for the economist's scepticism about the wisdom of the continental approach to water supply."

Water Supply concludes: "Development is not an intangible worthy of consideration as a goal in water supply projects over and above the economic consideration of costs and benefits. Rather, development in terms of exploitation of the real advantages of particular regions is best furthered by the construction of economic projects and by avoiding the waste of resources entailed by the construction of uneconomic ones."

A further consideration in the construction of the uneconomic projects that characterize water development is the absorption of large blocks of public capital that presumably could be used for other, and more efficient, public enterprises. It is often suggested that Canada needs American capital for development; if this is true, it would seem the better wisdom to use our own money for the economically sound investments that foreign capital would seek out, rather than sinking it into uneconomic, and often destructive water projects. If a growing economy is desired, there seems little point in pursuing it through money-losing water and power schemes.

It was typical of water development that as the Gardiner Dam was being completed, and as doubts as to its usefulness relative to its cost mounted, development boosters were pushing for consideration of yet further dams and diversions on the Prairies. Water could be diverted down the Qu'Appelle Valley to the Souris Valley, it was suggested; and the South Saskatchewan could be augmented by a series of diversions in Alberta, and by an aqueduct from the North Saskatchewan. There were all sorts of ways in which the water of Western Canada could be moved around, enthusiasts said. And so in 1967, the five-million-dollar Saskatchewan Nelson Basin study was inaugurated to see just what could be done with the rivers of the Prairies and the North. The final report on various combinations of 55 dams and 23 diversions is due for publication as this book goes to press. The environmental and social aspects of the

Saskatchewan-Nelson Basin study are discussed elsewhere in this book. As is so often the case, economics have no relevance in the study. No need has been established for the additional water that would be supplied to 18 arbitrarily picked points on the prairies by means of the dams and diversions envisioned by the study. The attitudes that brought us the Columbia Treaty and the South Saskatchewan project live on.

The omission of any study of water needs on the Prairies *before* initiating a study of dams and diversions to fulfill unknown requirements is so obviously an error that it is quite likely a "needs" study will follow. It will be very difficult to divorce it from the just completed Saskatchewan-Nelson Basin Study, however, because the whole history of water development suggests that projects are more the result of what *can* be done that what *needs* to be done. The Gardiner Dam is itself an excellent example of this. A study of water needs, then, at the very least must be totally divorced from the personnel and agencies who conducted the study of possible dams and diversions just completed. They could not possibly carry out a study which would not be predicated in part upon the combination of dams and diversions which they favour, and any report by such an agency would therefore be largely predictable, certainly highly suspect, and therefore totally useless.

A study of water "needs" is a job for economists, sociologists, and ecologists. Perhaps psychologists should be involved too, for as U.S. Geological Survey hydrologist H.E. Thomas has accurately pointed out: "Water shortage is a frame of mind." It certainly is of no value to suggest that "water if available in such a place could be useful for . . . [irrigation, industry, municipal use, or some combination] . . . and should therefore be provided." The point is that water "needs" must be directly related to the cost of providing that water. It might be nice to have a lake at Youngstown, Alberta, if it were free of cost. But if to accomplish it rivers have to be diverted, whole biological and social structures upset, and vast amounts of money spent, it seems unlikely that the lake should be provided. Perhaps three quarts of water per person are required each day for survival — beyond that point, water needs must be related to the cost of providing them.

So the question is not, "where could water be used if it were provided," but rather, "where is water the best answer to a need of the people in an area, how much of it can be supplied at a cost that is economically, ecologically, and socially much lower in cost than the value of the benefits to be gained?" To answer such a question requires studies that begin with the people and their needs, not with water. It requires that a whole range of alternative ways of meeting those needs be explored. Only if water is the best way of meeting those requirements should the variety of ways of providing water be examined. And that, as we shall see in Chapter 8, could be done in many ways other than through diversion from other basins or even through large scale development within the basin. If, finally, water development appears to be the best answer to the region's needs, careful studies of the costs and benefits to be attributed to the various ways in which development might be undertaken are required.

Though no Canadian studies of the cost of water diversions have yet been carried out, Americans Charles W. Howe and K. William Easter have studied just such activities and their costs in the United States. Their intensive investigation showed that the median cost of large interbasin transfers would be perhaps $50 to $60 per acre foot, with many such projects considerably higher in cost. Remembering that without supplying water for expansion of irrigated agriculture there could be no possible reason for moving water anywhere in North America, and that most farmers pay well below $5 per acre foot with $10 generally considered an absolute top that would allow for economic farming, the nature of the economics of water development begins to come into focus. Clearly, any suggestion that water be shifted from basin to basin in the Canadian west, or anywhere else in Canada, or exported to the United States, implies enormous subsidies of a nature totally indefensible if subjected to any sort of economic analysis. It becomes ever more clear — big dams mean big politics.

Water projects in the United States must be subjected to a "Cost-Benefit Analysis" before being approved by federal agencies. Presumably, the benefits must exceed the costs for the project to proceed. There is much to be said for such a procedure, and it is gradually receiving more use in Canada. The problem with such an analysis is that there is a great deal of latitude available to the person or organization doing the study as to the assumptions of what costs and benefits actually should be considered. There is as well the placing of evaluations on those factors that have been selected. And there is the question as to what is to be done with those factors which may be important but which defy quantification. The elimination of a way of life for a group of people is a common result of water development, for instance, yet because it is difficult to place a dollar value on it, such factors are normally just dropped from the calculations of costs and benefits. Aesthetic values and ecological factors often receive the same treatment. The difficulty of the situation is compounded by the fact that cost-benefit studies are normally carried out by the agency which has proposed and would expect to carry out the project if it is approved. With a stimulating project, along with careers and advancement at stake, it is too much to expect objectivity in the calculations.

Not surprisingly, then, the usual cost-benefit studies, a major factor in water development decision making, are seldom accepted at face value by observers outside the agency involved. American economist John Krutilla suggests why this should be the case in his country: "You have to understand that the water resources program in the United States is frequently referred to as the pork barrel . . . it's more politically than economically inspired and, as a consequence, since a large part of the development is not economic in any sense if realistically evaluated, it follows that the benefits are overstated and the costs minimized." Dr. Krutilla suggests that even minor water developments in the U.S. are for the most part questionable, and that large scale diversions are completely out of the question as an economic possibility. Here he is in accord with the authors of *Water Supply*, who suggest that the multi-billion dollar water development program of the United States Bureau of Reclamation would be practically eliminated if sound economic criteria were used. Dr. Derrick Sewell of the University of Victoria reports that, in Canada, "some provincial government agencies undertake benefit-cost analyses and so do a few agencies of the federal government. Many of those who undertake such analyses, however, do not adhere to the principles set out in the Guide, and in several cases the techniques have been grossly misused. A major problem, therefore, is that of increasing the level of sophistication of methods of evaluation used by government agencies and ensuring that such methods are correctly employed."

Resource economists are full of stories about the strange things they have found in examining benefit-cost studies carried out by water resource agencies. One of the most fascinating was found in a benefit-cost analysis of the Dos Rios project, a dam proposed as part of the State Water Project in California. Dos Rios was to be built by the Army Corps of Engineers, the other great water development agency in the U.S., on the Eel River. It would have flooded Round Valley, an Eden-like area of some 18,000 acres surrounded by dry mountains. It is one of California's most delightful human settlements, one in which the Indians who have long been there and the more recent white arrivals live in unusual harmony. According to the engineers, there is a possibility of floods costing an average of $36,000 in damage occurring in Round Valley. The Corps in its analysis said: "Round Valley would form part of the reservoir of the proposed project. Therefore, the project can be credited with the elimination of flood damage." And so a credit of $36,000 was added to the benefit side of the ledger—the Army Corps of Engineers would save Round Valley from floods by permanently inundating it far beneath the waves of their new reservoir!

Although this is an extreme example of misuse of cost-benefit figures, flood control is commonly a contentious issue in water development. The agencies wanting to build a dam are inclined to attribute high values to the protection of land and property downstream, often using the value of the damage that might be prevented as a "benefit." This of course takes no account of the fact that similar benefits might be achieved by other means at much less cost. Diking, for example, might be used to protect areas containing property of high value. More valuable would be proper flood plain zoning that would prohibit high density development on a flood plain, such as that of the Fraser River. Limiting the area to farming and other low density uses, and "flood-proofing" the buildings required for such activities, is a low cost intelligent approach to the management of flood-prone areas. Where government authorities are not prepared to follow such a program, the simple act of stamping all deeds to property within a flood plain with the designation, "flood plain", would serve to warn those who would buy land in the area what it is they are getting into. Real estate developers certainly do not generally tell prospective customers that they are buying homes or other buildings on land which was created by floods and can be expected to continue to have periodic floods. Flood insurance, warning systems, evacuation and relocation programs may seem last-ditch measures, but if people choose to live on a flood plain this approach, employed once in a number of years, would quite possibly make much more sense than the more simplistic but very expensive, and probably very damaging large dam.

The value attributable to the flood control aspect of a dam must be reduced as the risk is reduced by other means. For instance, in the area most prone to floods in Canada, the Fraser Valley, million of dollars have been spent on a diking system that will protect the area in all but the most severe flood situations. To claim full credit for flood protection for a dam on the Fraser would be indefensible. A similar situation existed on the Columbia River, where all three dams in Canada received proportionate credit for flood protection in the United States. In fact, the first dam accomplished by far the greatest part of the flood control and the last one contributed very little, since the first foot of flood protection is much more valuable than the last one. Properly attributing this figure might have made considerable difference in the benefit figures attributed to each dam and had the Columbia Treaty been in any way related to realistic economics, such a designation of costs and benefits might have made the system more economically sound.

A final observation with respect to flood benefits — historically, flood damage has increased in those areas for which flood control dams have been built. The reason is simply that no structure can be completely safe against the very large floods that come every century or so. Yet people are encouraged to develop a false sense of security, and they build extensively under what they assume to be the protection of the dam. And when the big one comes, there is much more property in its path to be damaged. This being the case, maybe dams should not have any flood control benefit attributed to them — perhaps the potential damage that the record so far shows will result from their construction should be charged against them!

Another fascinating benefit that the U.S. Army Corps of engineers often adds into its calculations, and one which we can expect to be imported into Canada, is called "land enhancement". Because as we have seen a dam has the effect of increasing real estate development pressure below the dam, the values of the land are bid up and this is claimed as a benefit for the dam. In the case of the San Luis Rey River project in California, 56% of the benefits of the dam were attributed to "land enhancement". No examples of this sort of thing are known to the author in Canada, but it is the sort of thing that might well be tried by an agency desperate to justify a water development project.

A first principle is clear with respect to benefit-cost analyses. They must never be the responsibility of any agency which has reason to be interested in seeing the project proceed. Even if done with meticulous care, it is so easy to lose all sorts of assumptions and omissions within the maze of figures that it would be difficult to accept even the most honest analysis. Such studies should be the province of an organization with the perspective and independence of an agency such as that of the Auditor-General in Ottawa.

Even with the best of intentions, benefit-cost is a tricky business. Economist James A. Crutchfield points out: "Even if you do benefit cost studies with utmost integrity and honesty . . . you are trying to project the pattern of regional and economic development 20, 30, perhaps 50 years in advance and that's something not easy to do . . . Somehow we seem to kid ourselves in planning water resources that we really know what's going to happen fifty or a hundred years in advance."

It is clear that we don't know what advances technology will make over such a period, except to be sure that they will be very great. Yet water development because of the enormous investment involved and the irrevocable nature of the physical structures locks society into today's technology for perhaps a century or more. Many of the biggest projects cannot even be opened and drained so they will have to be maintained even if they become useless. It is clear that the priorities and preferences of society are changing with extreme rapidity, yet the permanence of water projects ensures that the destiny of a river or a valley or a group of people is determined forever by decisions based on today's values.

University of British Columbia economist Michael Goldberg suggests that this represents the foreclosing of options for society, and that just as options are worth money in commercial transactions, so a value should be placed on the options foregone by society in proceeding with a water development project. "If a Fraser River hydro-electric dam destroys future alternate uses such as salmon, recreation, and farming, then the cost of having no future choices should be added to the cost of the dam." This is a cost additional to the cost which must be charged for lost opportunities represented by the dam. The multi-million dollar loss to the salmon fishery for instance must of course be added to the cost of the dam. Dr. Goldberg goes on: "I suspect, particularly with investments like large-scale hydro dams, that we do foreclose a large number of options. In a world of rapid population and economic growth I further suspect that these options are worth retaining. The cost of foreclosing these options should be included in the energy costs." Economist John Krutilla is so convinced of the importance of the value of retaining options that he suggests: "In future cases the value of retaining an option when faced with a decision having an irreversible result might be the critical element on which the decision would turn."

The question of opportunity costs in water development is one that receives considerable lip service but in reality is vastly underrated in benefit cost analysis. We will discuss in some detail later the implications for Canada of flooding many of the nation's finest valleys and the disruption of its great rivers. Because these things are hard to quantify, they are simply dropped from consideration in studying the feasibility of water development, though they may well include the most important long term consequences of proceeding with dams and diversions. There are however many opportunities foregone in river development which are simply ignored, though it would be quite possible to put values against them.

Consider once more the case of the Bennett Dam on the Peace River. It not only displaced the people and wildlife living in 680 square miles of magnificent wilderness where the Parsnip and the Finlay Rivers combined to flow through the Rocky Mountains as the Peace River; it also ended forever the possibility of logging in the river valleys where the soils are most fertile; no mines will ever extract whatever minerals now lie beneath the waves. The archaeology of the region is now a closed book, and the enormous recreational potential of the area is largely at an end since the Williston Reservoir behind the dam is unattractive and dangerous for this purpose. The economic loss represented by the elimination of the habitat of about 6,000 moose, large numbers of which could have been harvested each year by sportsmen forever, is just one aspect of the damage.

When the cost of the energy generated by the project is calculated, it does not include the loss represented by the drying up of two thousand square miles of the Peace-Athabasca Delta, several hundred miles downstream. The actual outlay on studies and technological first aid for the Delta is a small part of the real cost, yet not even that much is being attributed as a cost of the Bennett Dam.

This development provides an illustration of another sort of cost that is not included in benefit cost studies — the element of risk. This can take many forms. In the case of the Bennett Dam, three major law suits are pending against B.C. Hydro; by far the largest is for $30 million, brought by the consortium of construction companies who built the dam against Hydro to compensate for losses that they charge were due to mis-management by Hydro. The town of Peace River is suing for retrieval of $100,000 it claims the manipulation of the Peace River cost their community in rebuilding its water system. And the Indians of Fort Chipewyan are suing B.C. Hydro for the loss of their livelihood and way of life. In estimating the cost of the Bennett Dam, no allowance for the risk that such law suits might materialize was provided.

Another obvious risk in any project is that the estimates of costs and benefits will turn out to be incorrect, resulting in the failure of the project. "Failure of the project" can be defined as an outcome of the project in which an over-estimate of benefit or an underestimate of cost, or both, is sufficient to make the net balance of economic considerations negative. We have seen that historically the nature of cost-benefit studies has been such that "failure of the project" in these terms is a very real possibility in water development projects.

Then there is physical risk, which similarly is not found to be included as a cost in pre-construction estimates. The Mica Dam in British Columbia is an example of this; the reservoir is in an area of unstable rock formations and there exists the possibility that as the water level rises with completion of the dam, enormous rock slides could cause great destruction within the reservoir, or even overtop the dam. Some engineers and geologists privately feel the dam should have been another mile upstream to avoid some of the more serious slide possibilities. Remote though the slide dangers may be, they are possibilities, as the Vaiont Dam disaster in Italy in 1963 clearly showed. It is plain that even when the best men do the very best job possible, it simply is not possible to be sure of what might happen, nor is it possible to be sure of the effect of various occurrences. Luna B. Leopold of the U.S. Geological Survey is a hydrologist and engineer acknowledged as a world authority in the field. He states: "What engineers do is they pretend to be able to say that 'This is likely to happen', and that they can compute things. . . The fact is that our experience throughout the world has been that these forecasts have been so inaccurate, usually underestimating greatly the adverse effects."

The point is that risk exists, and the costs of some types of mishaps are enormous. The risk should be reflected in the cost-benefit analysis of any water development, and added to the cost of the water or power supplied by the project. This never occurs, and risks of all kinds are simply lost from consideration.

No examination of the economics of water development is possible without a discussion of discount rates. Though it can be confusing, the discounting of future costs and benefits is a relatively simple process. It is based on the idea that a benefit that will accrue some time in the future is worth less than the same benefit now. If you are paying for something now, you will want to pay less for it if you cannot reap the benefits immediately. And the longer you will have to wait, the less you will want to pay right now. Since water development characteristically involves spending a lot of money now for benefits that will be spread out over a long period of years, the rate at which these future benefits are discounted in an assessment of the economics of a project is very important. High interest or discount rates make projects look undesirable, and low interest rates make them look good. So it is normal to find water development agencies pressing for a low discount rate.

In fact, however, any discount rate lower than that found in the open market for investments of similar security, amounts to inefficient use of public funds. Since the interest rates of the market also reflect risk, a discount rate should also include a factor for this, as we have already shown. Together, such considerations would push the legitimate interest or discount rate on water development toward 10 per cent, suggests *Water Supply*. Other reputable economists and agencies agree.

Many fewer water projects would be built if such criteria of economic efficiency were used. As economist Kenneth Boulding once put it:

The long term discount rate
Determines any project's fate.
At two percent the case is clear;
At three some sneaking doubts appear.
At four it draws a failing breath,
While five per cent is instant death.

"Cheap" hydro electric power has been a tradition in Canada. It is now apparent that the only way in which it has been cheap is on the bills paid by consumers, and particularly by big consumers. Large industrial concerns have always had special privileges in this regard. To make "cheap" power possible, the user is charged a rate that will pay for the dams and generators and transmission lines, while the enormous environmental and social costs are absorbed by society. Full recognition of the extent of these costs has been to a considerable extent postponed for the next generation to discover, when the enormity of what has been done to the water resources of Canada will become obvious. Even the accounting applied to the physical structures themselves is highly questionable in many cases, as we have seen.

But there is another real cost associated with cheap hydro electric power. As the Conservation Foundation has put it, cheap energy has "encouraged technologies and practises that are highly energy-consumptive. This led to the evolution of an industrial society whose vital functions and economic institutions are premised on an ever-increasing rate of consumption. This consumption has been accompanied by serious and accelerating degradation of the physical environment" . . . and it might be added, by the certainty of depletion of many important resources. These are being consumed in a throw-away economy in which prosperity is measured by the amount of material extracted, processed, used, and somehow disposed of. Failure to properly cost our hydro-electric power development, then, has not only resulted in primary degradation of the environment, social disruption and economic innefficiency, but is closely related to broader questions of environmental deterioration and resource depletion.

In attempting to justify the construction of water projects, it is just as effective to add on benefits as to ignore costs. For instance, in recent years it has become fashionable to include large values for recreation benefits. The South Saskatchewan dam is a classic case in which such benefits have been used to justify a project. In a great many other Canadian reservoirs the dead and dying forests standing starkly in the water demonstrate the travesty of adding recreational benefits to dam construction projects in many cases. Even where proper clearing is carried out there is still the question of evaluating the new, flat water reservoir and the types of recreation common to such water. How do these compare with the aesthetic values of natural streams, and to wild river recreation such as hiking, stream fishing, or white-water canoeing?

Water development normally takes place in the most scenic areas of rivers where waterfalls and gorges and canyons occur, and where quality recreation can be enjoyed. The type of recreation made possible by a new reservoir is certainly not as pleasant as that to be found on a natural, nonfluctuating lake. Nevertheless, in sheer numbers, it may be possible to attribute more dollars to recreation in a reservoir (expenditures on boats, motors, and large numbers of people using them) than would be the case in recreation in the unspoiled environment of a wild river. This means that the list of benefits from the development proposal will be boosted in a way that takes no account of quality, nor affords any recognition of the loss of diversity and choice that is occurring as river after river is dammed. As Turner, Ahrens and Smith of the British Columbia Department of Recreation and Conservation have put it: "Quantity in terms of recreation visits may be gained at [the cost of] a loss in quality of the recreation experience."

Another benefit often cited is pollution control. By controlling the flow of the river, water can be released to flush pollutants downstream — in other words, the reservoir is to a river what the tank is to a toilet bowl. "The solution to pollution is dilution," those who cite this benefit of water development seem to be saying. Yet it is patently obvious that the only answer to pollution is to stop it — to process our wastes in such a way that the effluent discharged in our streams is not of a quality that requires "flushing". We know how to do it — it's a matter of getting on with the job.

The dilution of the domestic and industrial waste of the city of Edmonton is often cited as a major benefit of the Brazeau Dam in Alberta. Remarkable as it may seem, it is often suggested that additional fresh water diverted into the Great Lakes would be useful in flushing out those great bodies of water, even though the most rudimentary research shows this wouldn't work even if it were a desirable practice.

Any attempt to add benefits for waste disposal to a water development project should be forthrightly rejected. And the use of public funds to flush away the wastes of industries rather than requiring them to clean up their discharges, is certainly open to question.

Loading on benefits has become a standard practice by water development agencies in order to justify their projects. "Multiple-use" is the magic phrase, and the public is told that a dam will produce electrical energy, prevent floods, provide recreational facilities, perhaps water for irrigation, for municipal and industrial uses, and so on. The structure is usually given full credit for all of the many roles it is to play. Such a presentation of the function of dams is simply not in accord with the facts.

A dam has a principal purpose, and other values can be achieved only to a lesser degree than if the dam was primarily built for them. Some uses are quite incompatible. For instance, a hydro power dam should be kept nearly full in order to obtain all the energy that the water impounded behind it can deliver. A dam for flood control on the other hand should have its reservoir kept as empty as possible in order to contain flood run-off waters. Increasingly, hydro dams are used for "peaking" power, with base loads provided by thermal plants of various kinds. This means the water is kept high behind the dam, and when required for high load periods in the electrical system the generators can be started almost instantaneously and a great deal of energy can be generated over a short period of time. But this means a wildly fluctuating shore line, which is the factor most damaging to the use of a reservoir for recreational purposes. Downstream the river can be a trickle one hour and a torrent the next. Similar conflicts could exist between power and irrigation, or between other uses for which the dam is being promoted. It is, then, correct to attribute full value only to the prior use of the dam, with much reduced values attributed to any other possible uses. "Fundamentally, a dam cannot serve two or more masters at one and the same time and do a thorough job in all cases ... By and large there is a large gain, an expected one, in the particular use of the resource for which the project is designed. But just as evidently there is greater or lesser loss experienced by the other natural resources that are affected by the proposed project."

Beware of dam builders bearing multi-purpose water development projects!

Our final consideration in examining the economics of water development is perhaps the most important one of all. It is clear that environmental values are receiving much more consideration now than has been the case in the past. As each additional river is dammed, as each valley is flooded, as each waterfall is inundated, we are losing for ever "gifts of nature" that cannot be replaced. Further, it is obvious that with each wild river that is obliterated, those remaining have to be of greater value, since they are becoming relatively more scarce. The *second last* river is surely more valuable than the *second*, and a way must be found of showing this in our calculations. If we consider the river development proposals one at a time, we will dam them all, one at a time; and the total impact will not be evident until none of them survives in its natural state.

Our wealthy society is gaining in both appreciation of these natural features of our environment, and ability to take advantage of the recreational and aesthetic pleasures they provide. At the same time, the need for pursuing development of these rivers is diminishing. John Krutilla has done the seminal work in applying economic theory to this question and in trying to find ways of quantifying a question which is clearly vital. "When today we consider the development of say a hydro resource, or the reclamation of arid land, we find that technology affords us many alternatives for achieving the same objective. Moreover, technological progress has cheapened the cost of obtaining these same objectives by alternative methods. Consequently we can now give up some resource development activities that would pre-empt some of the aesthetic features of our natural environment ... we are also growing wealthier and can afford to forego the degradation of the natural environment to a great extent." In fact, if North American society, wealthiest the world has known, cannot afford this, no society possibly could.

Dr. Krutilla points out that while technology has shown alternative ways of generating power at lower cost, it will never be able to resurrect an extinct wildlife species, or reconstitute a destroyed wilderness. With greater appreciation and use of such resources, and a growing population, natural landscapes will increase in value with time while the technological use which has been made of them will depreciate in time as better technology is developed. It should also be added, that while the resource in its natural state will exist and be of value to man forever, water developments not only tend toward technical obsolescence but in a period of time — perhaps less than a century, perhaps a couple of centuries — the reservoir will have silted in and will be useless. Dams are temporary in usefulness; the destruction they cause is permanent.

The importance of this question is obvious, and yet it has been totally ignored in water development in Canada. Dr. Krutilla has done detailed economic analysis on the subject and shown how it can be brought into evaluations of water development proposals. Canadians should insist that these considerations be made an integral part of every water development proposed in this country.

It is quite clear that modern economics, including the aspects of it that have been discussed in this chapter, has had little application in Canadian water developments of the past. What is shocking however is that it is receiving no greater attention in new projects, and in fact the basic elements of economic analysis appear to be even more grossly violated in the biggest and newest projects, such as the Churchill-Nelson hydro project in Manitoba, and the enormous James Bay project in Quebec. Figures are not available that would make it possible for the public to assess the economics of these and other projects; the pattern of secrecy in Canadian water development continues.

Finally, it must be remembered that even when all the tools of modern economics are brought to bear on questions of water development, there will remain fundamental value judgements to be made by the people of Canada. Sound economic analysis is essential to provide information for the assessment of alternatives open to society, but many of the deepest questions surrounding the damming and diversion of Canadian rivers must be resolved in the end as questions of ethics and values, as these relate to the land and people of Canada. It will be necessary to assess the meaning of her free flowing waters to Canada as a nation, and to her people as individuals requiring the aesthetic and other satisfactions which only natural landscapes shared with other members of the biosphere can provide. It will be necessary to assess the importance of maintaining a diversity of land and water and people in the face of the "homogenizing" effect of great water developments.

Economic growth, though often more imaginary than real as we have seen, is the prime factor in water development promotion. Yet how long such growth can continue is perhaps the most fundamental question facing a society which has suddenly come face to face with the realization that we live on a finite earth; that nothing, not even our water resources, can be developed indefinitely. At some stage we will have to move into a type of economy more in equilibrium with our environment. We could consider doing that while there remains a rich and varied environment in Canada, rather than waiting until we are forced into it by a sadly demeaned and depleted land.

Chapter 7
Dam builders and dam boosters

Water has always been central to the concerns of men. A small amount of it — perhaps three quarts a day — is essential for human life. Larger quantities have been crucial in the rise and fall of great civilizations. In this century, many of the largest works of man are devoted to the management of water, and some of the greatest combinations of political power on the North American continent have evolved from the desire to manipulate rivers in one way or another. If some of the interests now at work prevail, the entire continent may be restructured to fulfill the imperative that many Americans and Canadians feel to have water flow in a way other than that which has evolved over thousands of years.

There is something strange about all this, something that cannot be explained by reason alone. It may in part be the fact of the absolute necessity for that first trickle of water to sustain life. Perhaps that imperative has been translated into a feeling that unlimited water is just as necessary, that life requires not merely that first three quarts, but indeed the entire one hundred and fifty gallons now used per person in many regions each day. It would seem by the rhetoric of water development enthusiasts that denying the last few gallons of that amount would be just as mortal a blow as witholding the first three quarts. There seems to be a widely-held myth, then, that man *must* have all the water he can possibly use, and it must be available at the lowest possible cost.

In earliest Biblical times, the control of water was much more important than possession of land. In fact, it was the wells that were privately owned in the days of Abraham, while the land was used in common by everyone. The situation was little different in the early days of the American West. From battles over waterholes for cattle, the conflict spread to the irrigation ditches which crept out across barren plains. California's Director of Water Resources William Gianelli points out: "Originally it started out with one fellow on a ditch stealing water from another and they would get into an argument and this would eventually perhaps result in a shooting and certainly in litigation. The area of conflict is a little different now. It's changed from those early days but I think it represents the same principle." Anyone who has observed the bitterness of the battles currently raging over water in California would certainly agree.

In Arizona, it is often said that water is a more emotional matter than sex. The governor of the state, Jack Williams, puts it this way: "If you're on a desert and the choice is death or how much would you pay for a drink of water, there's very little cost accounting — you'll pay anything for that cup of water. We are on the desert and if we don't get water death is the only other alternative. There is nothing else."

Now there is of course no question of Arizonans dying of thirst, since even at the present rate of withdrawal of their underground water supplies, there is enough to provide for 150 years. With wise use, they would probably last much longer. But the Governor's comment shows graphically how the desert and its obvious dryness, the history and folklore of pioneers who survived or died as a result of the presence or absence of a few gallons of water, has become an integral part of the outlook of many citizens of the American Southwest. This is particularly true of the older residents of the area. Over the years, that essential "cup of water" has grown to become a great aqueduct carrying water first from the Colorado River, then from the Columbia, and ultimately from Canada, into the heart of the state. That vital three quarts a day has become the $1.2 billion Central Arizona Project, and the $100 billion NAWAPA plan.

So all-pervasive has this modern mythology become that when a professor at the University of Arizona suggested to a Tucson service club that his studies indicated the state would be better off without importing more water, newspaper editorials and other pressures suggested that the university would be better off without his services. That is not surprising, perhaps, since sides have long since been drawn up on the issue. As Rich Johnson of the Central Arizona Project says: "In Arizona for years we have been keyed to fighting for the CAP against the opposition of our neighbouring states and it's become an emotional issue — in fact I sometimes think that some Arizonans weren't so much interested in getting water as they were in beating those people who oppose it." Within the state itself, northerners resent the fact that the rain falling on their more humid area has to flow south to the Phoenix-Tucson area. That's because the water was used there in earlier days, thereby establishing rights to it forever. And along the Colorado River, there are lands that could be irrigated but will not be because the CAP will require all of Arizona's share of the river; another cause of resentment. Then there is bitterness between farm and city — the urban areas reach out for water that lies under the farms, but are often prevented from doing so by state laws.

Attitudes are shifting in Arizona and other parts of the Southwest, however, with the influx of people who have not had a lifetime of exposure to the emotion of the issue, and who are not aware of any water problem at all in their personal lives. The academics and conservationists of the state who see no benefit, and even actual harm to the region from water importation, are gradually finding listeners. This factor seems to lead to increased pressure for water development by those who see the support for it gradually slipping away.

But while the myths and the battles over water in the arid regions of the Southwest are at the root of some of the growing pressures for the export of Canadian water, they do not explain the unbelievable pace of water development across the entire continent during the past half century, and in particular since the Second World War. It's necessary to dig deeper for the reasons underlying the headlong rush to dam and divert the waters of the continent with ever larger and more complex schemes.

Water planning is often the embodiment of the North American faith that resources are almost limitless in quantity; of the frontier philosophy that "over the hill there's more", whether it be land or trees or minerals or water. To many Americans, and some Canadians too, it is a logical progression of this idea that would carry the American search for more water north into Canada. Most Canadians would however halt such an ethic at the border, agreeing with General A. G. L. McNaughton in his description of the Columbia River Treaty and proposed water export schemes: "They are a means of allowing the United States to develop beyond the limit of its resources on the basis of those belonging to another country." Yet there is an identical spirit in Canada which would reach over into another watershed for water, and into the next, and the next, as is proposed in prairie water diversion projects, and in projects proposed in British Columbia, Ontario, and Quebec.

Part of the reason for treating our water resources as we do may be found in a characteristic which we share with the Americans. Gilbert White, of the University of Colorado is one of the continent's leading authorities in the field of water development, and with respect to the objectives underlying water development, he has said: "I would say that a dominant aim, although it's rarely been stated in the legislation, is to control nature. That is, there is a great temptation to man, once he knows he can manage some aspect of nature, to try to do so. And I would think that one would have to say that on some of our streams a dominant motive in building huge structures has been to control that river because we can do so. We have at times been carried away with the sense of our own power in being able to manipulate large river systems, whole networks of dams and reservoirs, levies, channel improvements. We have been so delighted with the opportunity to carry on this engineering work that we tend to forget why we're doing it. What the long term aims are we're trying to serve."

Raymond F. Dasmann has put it this way: "Americans have always shown a greater willingness to shape the land to suit their enterprise than to adapt their enterprise to the shape of the land . . . we prefer and find it cheaper in the short run to subdue nature rather than co-operate with it . . . we do not believe in adapting to environmental necessities. We demand that they be removed . . . Americans are impatient with the slow process of nature, with the normal events of biotic succession and change. They prefer the simplicity of a machine to the intricacies of a biota. The day-by-day problems of watershed management seem tiresome, whereas a large dam built to stop flooding 'for all time' has popular appeal."

It requires little involvement in the field of water resources to encounter those engineers and administrators who are honestly dedicated to the idea that dams in themselves are great benefactors of mankind. In the author's experience, examples are numerous. There was, for instance, a senior engineer long involved in dam design and construction in Canada who would not hear of the possibility that some water projects were other than totally beneficial. There was another engineer employed by an internationally known firm of dam designers whose eyes lighted as he described his favourite damsite on the Amazon River system — the construction of which would, in the opinion of some observers, be an unmitigated disaster. There was the consultant to the United Nations, who described how officials of U.N. agencies involved with water development would vigorously promote water projects around the world, particularly in underdeveloped countries. Yet experience is showing how such developments can be particularly unfortunate in struggling nations whose social and economic fabric can be torn apart by such projects.

Much of the modern dilemma in the water resource field may be attributed to our belief as a society in the ability of technology to solve any problem. It is true that science and technology have contributed mightily to our standard of material living in the western world. It is also obvious that technology has created many of the problems which are proving most difficult to solve, and increasingly we are recognizing that solutions do not always lie in the application of "more of the same". Garett Hardin has pointed out that there are classes of problems for which there is no technological solution. As we have seen and will explore further, many problems which are thought to be related to water belong to this category of problems with no technical solution. Attempting to solve them with dams or diversions or dikes may create even more intractable situations. The famed microbiologist Rene Dubos has said: "Technological fixes are at best short-range palliatives which usually create new environmental problems of their own . . . Technological fixes amount to little more than putting a finger in a bursting dike, whereas what is needed is a socio-technological philosophy of man in his environment."

Science has a vital role in helping us to understand our environment, and technology will continue to be of great help to man in future — but only if it is carefully controlled by society. It can no longer be allowed a momentum of its own, putting us in the position described by Ralph Waldo Emerson when he said, "things are in the saddle and ride mankind." In surveying the broad field of water development another comment by Dubos is appropriate: "When man truly enters the age of science he will abandon his crude and destructive attempts to conquer nature. He will instead learn to insert himself into the environment in such a manner that his ways of life, and technologies, make him once more at harmony with nature."

Much of the water development philosophy prevalent in Canada has been lifted almost unchanged from the American scene. The "errors" committed by nature in the location of rivers, and in their seasonal ebb and flow, is termed "maldistribution" by developers in both countries. They consider it a condition to be corrected. The PRIME program in Alberta, for instance, is almost identical in purpose and effect to the State Water Project in California. The Department of Water Resources in that state describes their problem this way: "The people have located themselves and their industries in such a way that 80 per cent of the water needs of California occur in the southern two-thirds of the state, while 75 per cent of the water supply is in the northern one-third of the state. California's water supply is adequate, but some of it needs to be redistributed."

Almost as an echo, Alberta's Water Resources Division says: "In addition to variations in water availability over the year, there are problems of water distribution throughout the province. The greatest requirements for water are in southern Alberta where irrigation, industrial, domestic and municipal demands are well established. The largest rivers, however, are in the north carrying their water to the Arctic ocean away from the centres of population. About 89 per cent of the total water flowing through Alberta is carried by these northward flowing rivers. The remaining 11 per cent which flow through the southern populated areas of the province must service 85 per cent of the population. The logical solution to this problem of distribution is to divert northern waters southward where they are more urgently needed."

The reasoning is identical. This "maldistribution," this determination to reshape the land to what some consider to be the convenience, indeed the right, of man, is the basis of water policy in California, in Alberta's PRIME program, the Saskatchewan - Nelson Basin Study and other water development programs in Canada. The "need" is considered self-evident — yet there is no stated requirement for water, no economic or social justification put forth, no consideration of ecological factors. It is postulated as a matter of simple faith that if there is more water in the north than in the south, and more people in the south than in the north, then water should be diverted south. In a complex age, an idea of such simplicity, innocent of any of the real issues to be faced in questions of water development, has a sort of charming naiveté. Unfortunately, it is also the rationale which underlies the great international water schemes which would ravage a continent and possibly destroy a nation: and it is the basic philosophy behind much that is worst in water development within Canada's borders.

It is often suggested that building water projects long before need is an economic procedure because inflation increases construction cost. It is only necessary to make two points here. First, if our economy continues to grow, a future generation will be much better able to afford these gargantuan engineering exercises than can this one, in the unlikely event that they should want them. And second, there is a great economic cost involved in building projects not presently needed, or in building them much larger than needed. This has been studied in detail by the Rand Corporation in the case of the Colorado Aqueduct, which brings water from the Colorado River to Southern California. Many years passed before the full capacity of the aqueduct was required. The "foresight" usually attributed to those who saw this project through in the 1930's is now viewed as having caused "a truly major economic loss to the region".

A 1961 study of the operations of the Metropolitan Water District of Southern California by the Center For Study of Responsive Law in Washington D.C. went even further. "The MWD has two basic functions: to obtain water, and to distribute it. The district has performed both with breathtaking incompetence from the beginning. It has arranged to obtain water only twice — when it decided to build the Colorado River Aqueduct in 1932 . . . and when it decided to buy State Water Project water in 1959. In each case, it has over-anticipated Southern California's demand for water by *decades*." The MWD, of course, has bitterly rejected the charge. But in fact, it is currently building facilities for an expected doubling of the population of Southern California, just as the region is showing signs of levelling off in growth, and indeed as people are beginning to flee the smog and freeways that have made the Los Angeles area a disaster. The MWD is one more example of how the long-held idea that "bigger means better and cheaper" which is so prevalent in water development circles is often in fact fallacious. In the case of Southern California it appears to have meant higher taxation for the population and cheap water for a favoured few; it is a philosophy which extends into Canada with the continued insistence on the need for more water in the United States. It is the type of thinking behind the Saskatchewan-Nelson Basin Study.

A good deal of the thrust for ever more water development, both in Canada and internationally, is the insistence upon regarding water as essentially a "free good": that like air, it should be available as desired by everyone. No one should be denied free access to the water required for life, of course, but beyond that it is misleading to consider water in any sort of mystical terms. For it costs money to dam and divert and pipe and provide water for users, whether for domestic or industrial or agricultural purposes. As we have seen, traditionally water has been supplied at prices much below even this cost, and in part this must be because of the mystique of water and the reluctance to regard it as an economic commodity.

The mythology of water is a subject which could be discussed at great length. Many aspects of water development that could fall into this category are discussed in other parts of this book. However, these few examples of myths and emotions prevalent in water development raise an interesting question. Who is responsible for perpetuating them? How is it that the public can usually be counted upon to foot the bill for these great water developments which are at the same time the largest and most questionable public works programs in history? Politicians come and go, but seemingly only the faces change, for the policies proceed almost unaltered. Manitoba provides a particularly graphic example of this. The government of Premier Edward Schreyer came to power in part at least because of promises carefully to re-examine hydro development policies in that province. Within a short time, the government was proceeding with essentially the same water policies as its predecessor—an example of the way in which water development policies continue virtually unchanged even thought the actors in the drama are replaced from time to time.

The continuing elements in the field of water development are the agencies which plan and carry out the work, the lobbies or groups of various kinds which support and promote their activities, and those groups which stand to benefit economically from water development — construction firms, engineering consultants, land speculators and developers, irrigation interests, and so on. Those who will profit by development are usually to be found in the membership of the groups which support the water development agencies. Such associations are usually a combination of individuals who have been convinced that there is validity in the mythology of water development, and those who stand to gain financially from it. There are also those who take membership in such groups not recognizing the real purpose of the organization, since membership is often solicited under various "God and motherhood" statements of purpose.

It is somewhat simpler to sort this out in the United States than in Canada. South of the border much more water development has been carried out and the pattern is clear. By far the most of it is done by two large agencies of the federal government. They are the U.S. Army Corps of Engineers, and the Bureau of Reclamation. The Bureau is restricted to projects which have some relationship to irrigation, while the Corps spends almost one and a half billion dollars annually building water development projects for navigation, flood control, generation of power and any number of other purposes. Its civilian activities are carried out by a bureaucracy of 32,000 civilians under the direction of 200 military officers. More than 10,000 people are employed by the Bureau of Reclamation. Although almost every river of consequence in the United States has already been manipulated in some way, the Corps and the Bureau insist that ever greater water development is essential. It is of course in large part the survival instinct at work. As long as the dams go up, the agency is assured of extended life, and its personnel will enjoy job security.

It is not surprising, then, that Elizabeth B. Drew, writing in the *Atlantic* magazine in April of 1970 found that "the Corps has mastered the art of convincing people that its projects are desirable, and so the projects are not examined very closely. Corps engineers are impressive in their command of details that non-engineers cannot understand, assiduous in publishing books that show what the Corps has done for each state, and punctilious about seeing that all the right politicians are invited to each dedication of a dam." Dr. Bret Wallach of the University of Victoria has studied legal and administrative aspects of water development, and he finds that in the U.S. the real decisions on water developments are made before they reach Congress, and that all the democratic process can do is slow down the inevitable.

A large number of organizations work hard at ensuring that the plans of the Corps and the Bureau are brought to fruition. The National Rivers and Harbours Congress lobbies for the Corps, and the Bureau of Reclamation has as its own private lobby the National Reclamation Association. Various groups spring up as required to push particular projects or groups of projects, and invariably they are generously financed and able to afford well-staffed permanent offices, quite spectacular public relations campaigns, and the skilled political manoeuvering required in state and national capitols. Examples are the Central Arizona Project Association whose objective is obvious, and the Colorado River Association which is dedicated to the acquiring of ever more water for southern California.

In Canada, the situation is quite different in that the provinces have much more responsibility for water development within their borders than do the states in the U.S. and so the key agencies are provincial water resources divisions, under a variety of titles, and the hydro electric authorities. The Federal government becomes involved when rivers flow through two or more provinces or across an international border, or when proposed projects are larger and more uneconomical than a province can sustain on its own. The Gardiner dam in Saskatchewan is an example of this.

A clue to the attitude of water resource agencies is to be found in an Alberta Government publication relating to that province's plan for manipulation of almost all its rivers. "PRIME is a program conceived by the Water Resources Division, Alberta Department of Agriculture, to guide the development of the province's water resources." PRIME was adopted in all its far-reaching ramifications by the Social Credit Government of Premier Strom without public discussion. Neither biologists nor other professionals concerned with the social impact of PRIME were involved in the project prior to its adoption.

The highly respected head of Alberta's Water Resources Division, Reginald Bailey, considers that the role of his agency is to ensure that, "whatever social or economic development society determines for itself, it is our responsibility to ensure that water is not a deficient ingredient." This is of course precisely that North American preference discussed earlier that would force the natural world into the shape we would prefer in order to attain short term objectives. It ignores the distinct possibility that it might be preferable to work *with* the land and water, rather than to remold them in accordance with current whims.

Jack Hirshleifer and his co-authors of *Water Supply* in observing the work of water agencies note: "There is a certain temptation for water supply leaders to cast themselves in heroic mold as mighty battlers for the cause of pure and adequate water. To maintain the romance of this role, great projects are continually being conceived, planned, and executed, some of these schemes being sound, others unsound, and some bordering on the manic. As compared with such dreams and schemes the possibility of improving the efficiency of water use by such unromantic devices as elimination of waste or rationalization of pricing procedures may seem drab indeed — the more so as the large gains achievable by merely making better use of supplies in hand may indicate postponement indefinitely of vast new engineering wonders."

The persistence of water development agencies in seeing their dreams to fruition is remarkable. It has often been pointed out that once a water plan is given life, it never seems to die. It may be shelved temporarily when conditions are not favourable for its adoption, but it invariably reappears when resistance has faded. Studies of water development schemes seem to re-enforce one another; once a project is proposed, it re-appears in subsequent studies which may be undertaken for quite different agencies. This has been the case with PRIME in Alberta — shelved by the present government, it lives on in the Saskatchewan-Nelson Basin Study.

Once the data for a project exists, it is much easier to use it than to start from scratch with new information, or with a totally new approach to the water problems of an area. And of course, all this planning and study activity has to result in the occasional birth of a project if the continuation of the agency is to be justified. If dams and diversion are studied and planned, dams and diversion will eventually be built. General McNaughton put it this way: "It is my experience that once such matters appear on the agenda, and money is spent on studies, then vested interests appear, and often there is no stopping them." The evident truth of this is a strong argument against the endless "feasibility" studies which proceed to find ways of manipulating water prior to establishment of any demonstrable need.

An example of the determination with which water projects are followed through is the State Water Project of California. It began with a 1956 report on preliminary studies as to how all the rivers of California might be developed for various useful purposes, a report remarkably similar in purpose to that of Canada's Saskatchewan-Nelson Basin Study released in the fall of 1972. By 1972, water from

Northern California was flowing into the Los Angeles area of southern California through the facilities of the biggest water diversion system in the world. Between those dates, and continuing now, an extremely bitter battle has been waged over the project, its cost, its environmental impact, the profits of land speculators, and its social impact.

It is a typical "stair-step" development. As water from northern rivers is diverted to the southern part of the state, problems are created in the Sacramento-San Joaquin Delta, through which that water normally flows to the sea. A great agricultural and recreational region near San Francisco, the Delta requires the flow of fresh water through it to prevent salt water from the ocean moving inland and destroying the Delta. The answer, according to the developers, lies in more water from more northern rivers, and a great canal carrying northern water around the Delta. Conservationists and a large part of the population of Northern California simply do not believe the protestations of the water developers and the government that these developments can proceed without further damage to the Delta and the life within it. They fear the damming and diversion of the last of the free flowing rivers of northern California will be carried out in order to provide an ever larger flow of water into the desert lands owned by great corporate landholders, and to provide for ever greater urban growth in areas already hopelessly congested.

The financial and environmental problems of the project could have been predicted, and in fact they were. The state government in 1958 appointed an independent Board of Consulting Engineers to review the project, and it found parts of the plan inadvisable. Even before the Board reported to the government, political decisions were made to proceed, and estimates were publicised that bore no relation to the work of the Board. As soon as legislation approving the project was passed, the Board was discontinued and asked to restrict the scope of its report. Even so, the limited report of the Board was reported in the San Francisco *Chronicle*: "State Water Plan called impossible. Experts point out illegal, impractical proposals by [Governor] Brown." A member of the Board, internationally recognized consulting engineer Adolph J. Ackerman, submitted a minority report stating: "No conventional demonstration has been made of the financial feasibility or justification for the project, and no clearly engineered concept has been presented which may be considered as valid and as in the public interest."

Another review committee which included such eminent people in the field of water resources and economics as Gilbert White and Kenneth Boulding didn't last long enough to file any kind of a report. As Dr. Boulding put it a few years later: "Gilbert and I were on a committee supposed to be advising California on water some time ago. When they found out what the committee was going to say, they abolished it."

The California experience is particularly interesting because it provides a precedent with which to compare current Canadian experience. It was justified for precisely the same reasons given for the diversion plans being studied in Canada, it cost far more than had been officially predicted, a lot of effort went into keeping facts from being widely distributed, and independent agencies that might have helped in reaching rational decisions were emasculated when it appeared their recommendations might not be in accord with decisions already reached. All of this bears a striking resemblance to the current pattern of water development in Canada.

We have seen in earlier chapters that other lessons of the California experience could be observed closer to home. The Columbia River Treaty, for instance, is a Canadian tragedy in economic, social, and environmental terms, and a study of the growing literature on the subject shows quite clearly that the myths of water development along with institutional and political rigidity and ambitions were responsible for it. Dr. Derrick Sewell points out that: "The bargaining [between the U.S. and Canada] became so tough that once a point had been won there was little chance that further negotiation could take place even though the latter might lead to a more advantageous position for both sides." This seems to be a key reason for the flooding of the Arrow valley, an action that we saw in chapter 6 was not necessary to fulfill the terms of the treaty. It is clear also that the real reason for the building of the Libby dam in Montana, which floods 40 miles of magnificent Canadian valley land, can only be the decades-old determination of the U.S. Army Corps of engineers to build the project.

In Saskatchewan, it is doubtful if the economically disastrous Gardiner Dam would have become politically profitable had it not been for the promotional activities of the Prairie Farm Rehabilitation Administration, heartily backed by the Western Canada Reclamation Association, now the Canadian Water Resources Association. And it is all being repeated, over and over again, from one coast to the other. James Bay, Churchill-Nelson, Iskut-Stikine . . . rapidly accumulating understanding of the economic, environmental and social aspects of water development so far plays an infinitesimal role in decision making when compared to institutional and political pressures that are not really related to water at all.

U.S. water development agencies have come under increasingly vigorous attack as one by one the last of the wild rivers are plugged, and as plans are unveiled for the flooding of some of the last great wilderness valleys in that country. Large-circulation magazines carry articles like "Dam Outrage: The Story of the Army Engineers", and "The Public Be Dammed", in which U.S. Supreme Court Justice William O. Douglas says, "The Army Corps of Engineers is Public Enemy number one." Books such as *The Diligent Destroyers* and *America the Raped* take a predictable approach to the works of the dam builders. Back in 1965, Paul Brooks was a little more subtle when he wrote in the *Atlantic:* "As any small boy knows, the presence of running water is a compelling reason to build a dam. Most boys when they grow up turn to other things but a select few go on to join the U.S. Army Corps of engineers. Here, under the heading of flood control, navigation or power production, they build dams beyond the wildest dreams of youth. Some of these dams are necessary and some are not; all of them provide jobs for the Engineers. Most of them involve huge expenditures of federal money."

The expansion of the irrigated acreage of the western U.S., the function of the Bureau of Reclamation, is increasingly recognized as ludicrous. The Bureau therefore is being widely regarded as a dinosaur which long since completed any useful role it had to play. Perhaps its attempt to build two dams within the Grand Canyon to generate power to help pay for the Central Arizona Project jolted the American public into a realization of the sort of thing was being perpetrated in the name of reclamation. The Grand Canyon fight was probably the greatest American conservation battle to that time. Conservationists turned the tide against the powerful forces that wanted the dams as the initial step in financing successive water diversions, and the proposal was dropped in 1968. The battle pitting conservationists against water development agencies continues across the U.S.

In Canada, opposition to water development plans has become vigorous more recently. Proposals for the damming of the Fraser River at Moran Canyon put forth in the 1950's were defeated at that time largely on economic grounds — the loss to the fishing industry would be great. When the same proposal became a live issue again in 1970, the ensuing battle took place on a much broader front. The total environmental and social impact of the damming of this great river became an issue, not just the dollars that would be lost by the fishing industry, although this too was considered important. Though public opposition to the project seems overwhelming, the issue is not resolved as this book goes to press. Much depends upon a report of the B.C. Energy Board, being released in the fall of 1972.

Conservationists fear that the report will recommend many other dams in B.C. if it does not recommend Moran on the Fraser. It will be said that the construction of dams on tributaries of the Fraser will protect the Fraser Valley from flooding. If these were built, it would encourage further real estate development in the Valley — development which will be inundated when a really big flood occurs, as it must some year. Neither upstream dams or Moran can prevent that. The extreme damage resulting will arouse a public demand for, or acceptance of the Moran Dam, in the mistaken belief that it would be an ultimate solution to Fraser Valley flooding. Construction of Moran would be followed by many more dams on the Fraser and its tributaries.

If this scenario is followed, B.C.'s great rivers will be only a memory, and the salmon will be an epicurean delicacy of the past, a miracle of nature living only in legend. And it will have happened because the people of the province are not being told the truth about the Fraser Valley flood plain, and because greed is being allowed to prevent proper regulation of development on the plain. The Fraser will be blamed for disasters created by politicians, land and water developers, and B.C. Hydro.

Great opposition to the Churchill diversion into the Nelson River was a political issue in Manitoba in 1971, and will likely be so again. The "Damn the Dams" group in Northern Ontario is vigorously opposing dams and diversions being proposed in that province, and "The James Bay Committee" in Quebec is fighting that enormous development along with the Indians of the province. Conservationists in Alberta feel their province was sold short by the Social Credit government when it went ahead with the Big Horn Dam, and they are prepared to fight harder to prevent similar developments in future. And so it goes, right across Canada.

Lobbies supporting water developments in Canada have not achieved the size and sophistication of those in the United States. Probably the most important one is the Canadian Water Resources Association. Its membership includes individuals and corporations, and it appears to support any sort of water development as being for the public good. Originally formed to support irrigation in western Canada, it has backed such developments as the Gardiner Dam in Saskatchewan, the Columbia River Treaty, the Saskatchewan-Nelson Basin Study, and the St. Lawrence Seaway. In a brief to a House of Commons Committee concerning the Canada Water Act, the CWRA in 1970 urged increased federal involvement in water development, including the establishment of a Canadian Reclamation Bureau, acceptance as federal policy of the construction of uneconomic water projects, and federal acceptance of the principal of continental development of Canadian water — that is, the export of Canadian water to the United States.

Apart from such briefs, the CWRA has not formally adopted into its constitution the advocacy of water export, but several of its officers have spoken favourably of it on numerous occasions, the pages of its official publication devote a great deal of space to those advocating export, and those favouring such developments are prominent at the annual conventions of the Association. Since the purpose of the CWRA is to "promote the greatest use of all our resources of land and water for the greatest good, for the largest number for the longest time", it has drawn into membership many who are not perhaps totally aware of the actions of the organization. Statements, publications and programs of the organization show little evidence of any understanding of modern water management principles. Certainly there is no sign of a sophisticated approach to the economic, environmental or social issues involved.

The water development agencies are largely manned and directed by engineers, men trained to use modern science and technology for the benefit of mankind. Inevitably, then, they are caught in the middle at this time of changing attitudes toward technology. Engineering Professor S. O. Russell of the University of British Columbia says: "Since, of all professionals, civil engineers have been most conspicuously involved in the impact of man on the environment, they are now probably considered as the group most responsible for its problems, and consequently feel themselves to be very exposed . . . they have, until recently, enjoyed mild approbation, but suddenly they are now under widespread and increasing criticism. Not surprisingly, they are bewildered and uncertain."

For the past century or so, the engineer has been an almost heroic figure in our society. He pushed our great buildings skyward, carved our transportation routes through the mountains, vaulted wide rivers with bridges of steel and concrete. More recently, however, the emphasis has been upon halting those rivers in their channels, creating lakes and diversions, generating power. As Dr. Peter Larkin has put it somewhat irreverently: "The young engineers of the 19th century graduated with visions of the bridges they would build, while those of the 20th century were full of dam nonsense."

While engineers are the prime promoters and builders of dams, it would be totally incorrect to infer that battle lines are drawing up, with engineers on one side and biologists, conservationists and other members of society on the other. Some of the most enlightened leadership in modern water management is coming from engineers, men such as Professors Cass Booy and Robert Newbury of the University of Manitoba or Dr. Luna Leopold in the U.S. Consider this statement by the Dean of Engineering at the University of British Columbia, Dr. W. D. Liam Finn, and Professor S. O. Russell of the same faculty.

Major dams pose special problems since they are to all intents and purposes permanent. Unlike, say, obsolete canals, they cannot be allowed to fall into disuse and disrepair but must be maintained in fully operable condition. In making the decision to build a dam, therefore, it is necessary not only to evaluate the benefits and costs over the range of probable outcomes within the context of today's values, but over the range of possible future value systems. Otherwise we may construct projects which appear highly desirable now but may turn out to be totally inappropriate in the light of tomorrow's values. The problem of evaluation is compounded by the trend to larger and hence more permanent dams. With large dams even the immediate effects are often ex-

tremely difficult to predict, let alone benefits and costs over a long period of time and within a reference system which is continually changing.

But it must be admitted that such men are not yet nearly as influential as those who consider it an imperative to press on with "development" of our rivers as being a self-evident good. In his survey of attitudes and perceptions of water resource engineers, Dr. Derrick Sewell found: "Their views seem to be highly conditioned by training, adherence to standards and practices of the respective professions, and allegiance to the agency's or firm's goals or mission. Both groups (water engineers and health workers) believe they are highly qualified to do their respective jobs, and that they act in the public interest. Contact with representatives of other agencies or the general public, however, is considered either unnecessary or potentially harmful. There appears to be general satisfaction with past policies and practises, and few if any major alternations are suggested."

This profile of water resource engineers as seen in Dr. Sewell's British Columbia survey helps to explain much that is currently occurring in Canadian water resource development, and why changes that are so desperately needed are painfully slow in being considered, let alone implemented. He found that while the younger members of the profession were more concerned about such things as environmental degradation and public involvement, they felt quite powerless to do anything about these things. The older engineer, occupying a senior position, "has a fairly narrow view of problems facing society, and identifies solutions in terms of the conventional practise of his agency . . . Seniority brings with it an increasing degree of dedication and commitment to the agency." Since the interests of the agency are, as we have seen, often quite different from those of society generally, this is a serious situation. It is particularly so since successive governments seem ready, after a period of steady indoctrination by senior water resource and hydro officials, to proceed with the policies of which they once were critical. This has occurred in a particularly vivid way in Manitoba, and it seems possible that the new Conservative government of Alberta may not be far from agreeing to the study of interbasin transfers, after vowing never to do so when taking office.

Many engineers in various water development agencies are

faced with difficult choices, even "crises of conscience" on many occasions. As we will see later, this is often because they have been told clearly that they must say nothing about their work and their attitudes toward it, even though they are supposed to be functioning in the public interest. But their silence and lack of influence on the course of events in their field is often imposed voluntarily upon themselves under the guise of "professional ethics". Unfortunately, the ethics involved are often not those that would protect the real client, the public, in water resource issues. Rather, such rules protect the client who happens to be signing the checks, even though public money is being used for the purpose. An example in the personal experience of the author relates to the potential that exists for enormous rock slides into the Mica Reservoir on the Columbia River. Since the possibility had never been publicly acknowledged and was obviously a matter for public concern, research was undertaken for a television program on the subject. The program was produced, but it suffered from a lack of public statements by engineering geologists familiar with the site and its problems. Several were approached, in government, university, and private practise, and most agreed the matter was one about which the public should be informed. But they all stated, for a variety of reasons, all related to some question of "ethics", that they could not personally speak publicly on the issue. Many expressed the hope however that one of their professional colleagues would do so.

For many engineers, this sort of thing is just not good enough. They view their responsibilities more broadly, in keeping with a statement of the American Society of Civil Engineers which begins: "Professional engineers have given an oath to serve the public interest above all others." The respected consulting engineer Adolph J. Ackerman has said, "The individual engineer, and particularly the independent consulting engineer, commits himself to *serving the public interest above all others* and carries this responsibility on his conscience." To those who would insist that this responsibility is discharged by using his engineering skills to build sound structures in accordance with the best of engineering technology, Ackerman says: "The administrative engineer who assumes a public responsibility also assumes the duty to give the public all the facts and to oppose any misrepresentation of his services. Under this personal commitment it is his duty to communicate both the palatable and the unpalatable facts to the public through responsible media of publicity."

There are in Canada a few engineers who have understood and with great courage carried out this aspect of their responsibility to the people of the nation. Many more, regrettably, identify so closely with their agency as to see its welfare their prime responsibility. Perhaps, as Dr. S. O. Russell suggests, "Engineers need a new ethic."

As we try to find, in our myths and our institutions, reasons for our behavior in the field of water resource development, we should not overlook the possibility that the explanation for much of what we are doing is really quite simple. Dr. Frank Quinn puts it this way: "The brief history of man on earth suggests precedents and lessons for modern water engineering. It is apparent from a reading of the great civilizations, for example, that pharoahs, emperors, and monarchs shared a common aspiration to be immortalized in huge construction projects; and how better to write one's name across the earth than by changing the course of rivers, lopping off the tops of mountains, or digging vast canals? Similar aspirations are inferred to be rife even today among the planners and constructors of great water projects. This might account for the sense of mission unmistakable in many of the proposals recently volunteered for large scale diversions."

This "Pyramid Syndrome" is rampant all over the world. In the United States most dams, canals, pumping stations and even such mundane installations as filtration plants bear the names of the administrators who pushed the projects, or the politicians who helped nurse them through legislatures.

In his typically irreverent way, Kenneth Boulding has suggested: "The only way you could explain the water policy in this country was the religious explanation that we worship the water goddess, and hence had to build all these pyramids — all these dams and temples. There is no other conceivable rational explanation."

Dr. Gilbert White, one of the world's great authorities in the field of water resources, left his position at the University of Chicago to head up a new "Institute of Behavioral Sciences" at the University of Colorado. The author once asked Dr. White why he had done so, and in retrospect, it was a very naive question. The whole question of water development has a great more to do with human behavior than it has to do with water. Probably it will only be possible to understand why we do what we do with this most precious resource when we know a good deal more about man and the reasons for his activities; certainly his performance with respect to water has been and continues to be most remarkable.

Chapter 8

Water management: the alternatives

We have seen how water development generally occurs as a simplistic answer to a problem that may or may not actually exist. It normally is the product of promotion by various groups and institutions which usually stand to gain from the development in one way or another. In exploring this question of water development, many alternative ways of approaching the expressed "need" for water or energy have become obvious. In this chapter we will try to summarize some of the alternatives to massive water development that might be more in keeping with the real requirements of Canadians, and that are in keeping with our understanding of the nature of water and land. Considerable attention will be paid to possibilities that exist in the United States for alternative approaches to water supply problems, since that is where growing demand for Canadian water will originate. But the principles involved are equally applicable to Canadian situations, and should be considered when water diversion within the borders of this country is proposed.

This subject is difficult to approach because of the problem of deciding what the "need" for water really is in any given situation. We have discussed this in some detail in the previous chapter. Here we will explore various alternatives that could be considered in meeting various levels of need, and also ways in which those expressed needs might themselves be re-examined. These alternatives could be broadly grouped as economic, technological, and social approaches to the supply of water and energy.

Some interesting contradictions lie at the root of water and energy supply problems. Shortages of water occur largely because there is so much of it, circulating from ocean to atmosphere to streams and lakes and back to the oceans; and from the related fact that water is delivered to the user for so low a price. "Water is common, easily accessible, and cheap. It is cheaper than dirt; you can buy water in our cities, delivered to your bath and sink, for about a nickel a ton, while just ordinary dirt fill costs from a dollar up, and topsoil comes at around $10."

In a society that puts a dollar value on just about everything, the result of low prices for water is predictable. Waste. Waste is rampant in almost every use to which water is put. We know that without at least certain minimum quantities of water life is impossible, but because it is so cheap the consumer places little value on it, and waste in urban water systems, in industry, and in irrigated agriculture is enormous. Strangely, the common toilet still uses up to 6 gallons per flush, when 2 should be all that is needed. Modern technology should surely be able to do better than this with a common device that, with better design, could save enormous quantities of water.

The City of New York provides one of the most blatant examples of wasted water, as we saw in chapter 1, and many economists insist this is because of the low price charged for that water. The pattern of maintaining water prices below real cost is a typical practise in those areas which are most vociferous in pleading shortages, and which cry out for other areas, such as Canada, to bail them out by shipping in water. Water prices in 1960 in the Los Angeles area were 35% lower than an average of 500 U.S. cities. The Metropolitan Water District of Southern California, which supplies water to more than 100 cities in that state, charges users much less than the cost of bringing water to them. The difference is made up through property taxation, effectively removing constraints from those using large quantities of water.

Industries of all kinds use water at wildly varying rates. "A kilowatt hour of electricity generated by steam turbines takes as little as 1.3 gallons of water at some power stations and as much as 170 gallons at others. In some steel plants more than 25,000 gallons of water are required in the production of a ton of finished steel, while at other plants only 1,400 gallons are needed for the same purpose. Requirements in the production of a pound of artificial rubber range from 13 gallons to 300 gallons." Similar comparisons can be made between efficient and wasteful pulp mills; or between aluminum smelters where water requirements for a pound of aluminum range from 1.24 gallons to over 36 gallons; or oil refineries, some of which may use as little as 1.73 gallons of water to refine a gallon of crude petroleum, while others consume as much as 44.5 gallons of water. Clearly, there exist enormous opportunities to use water much more efficiently in industry. Yet: "It is not uncommon for municipal water sold for industrial purposes to decrease in price as the quantity increases. This promotes inefficiency and leads to a discrimination in favor of industries which find it convenient to use a great deal of water."

In agriculture, the nature of the use of water is such that the percentage of it that can be saved through avoiding waste is less than we have noted in other industries. Yet because farming absorbs 90 per cent and more of the water that is used in many of those areas of the United States which want to import Canadian water, any savings through increased efficiency of water use are enormously important in absolute terms. For instance, the All-American canal which carries 4 million acre feet of water from the Colorado River to the Imperial Valley is unlined, and seepage through its walls is an important cause of loss. So are the unlined ditches leading to farm fields across the burning desert. Much more is lost from evaporation into the dry hot air. It is estimated that the dry-land farmers of the West lose twice as much water in evaporation to the air as is taken from streams and wells and springs for distribution to all the public waterworks in the United States.

Clearly, water use in North America is characterized by waste in all of its manifestations. This waste seems most notable in those areas which most frequently propound their need for importation of water from other parts of the United States, and eventually from Canada. So it is obvious that what they are looking for is not just water; what they really are driving for is more *cheap* water — water that would be cheaper than the cost of making more efficient use of the water they already have.

As noted earlier, industrial use of water varies greatly in efficiency. Realistic pricing of water is the simplest way of encouraging water conserving processes, recycling, and other efficiencies. Since inefficient use brings closer the day when new facilities will be required to provide more water for the region, a "stepped" pricing system might encourage more efficient use of water. For instance, a realistic present cost might be involved in pricing water used up to the amount known to be reasonable for the state of the art of that industry. Consumption beyond that point might be charged at a higher level commensurate with the probable higher cost of providing new sources of water for the region.

A similar principal can be applied in the case of energy

supplied by hydro-electric dams. If the true cost of the power were charged to consumers, and if, as has been often suggested, electricity charges went up with increased consumption rather than down as is normally the case, industrial and domestic users of power would strive for increased efficiency in the use of electricity. The energy industry is one where increasing costs prevail, with each new generating unit costing more than the previous one. Prices reflecting this fact would include the cost of the *next* generation unit, rather than the last one constructed.

With the introduction of realistic pricing for water and energy, a great many alternatives to water development projects will receive the attention they deserve. First, it can be expected that requirements will be reduced in domestic, industrial, and agricultural uses as waste is reduced, and more efficient use made of water and energy. Homeowners will repair leaking taps and toilets, and water lawns more judiciously. Industries will concentrate on proven and innovative methods of recycling water, rather than paying for the much larger quantities involved in "once-through" systems. Irrigation will tend to be used for high value crops, with the grains and forages that are dependent upon artificially low water prices being reduced in acreage, making water available for users who can pay for it.

It is often suggested that the continued and expanded irrigation of the arid areas of North America is a necessity to help feed a hungry world. Books have been written on this subject alone, but a few points emerge from the debate as it applies to the need for irrigated agriculture in the U.S. and Canada, particularly when the manipulation of water systems is involved. First, it is generally agreed that it is not possible to feed the enormous numbers of people in those countries where hunger is an ever-present reality by importing large quantities of food from distant lands on a continuing basis. The logistics of such an operation would be physically and economically insupportable. Add to that the very high real cost of irrigating arid lands for this purpose, and "making the desert bloom to feed the starving millions" becomes an unreasoned fantasy.

It is clear that the only hope of overpopulated and undernourished nations is in programs of birth control and improved agriculture within their own borders. Both are enormously difficult to implement, and the introduction of newer farming techniques is proving to be fraught with many complicating factors. Yet only in these directions can hope be expected in these nations.

At the present time, some 50 million acres of American farmland is being held out of production under various price suppport programs. This would indicate that the provision of new land for agriculture through massive irrigation projects is hardly a matter of first priority. Should a revolutionary change in American policy require that more food be grown than is presently the case, there is much that can be done even after all this retired land is brought back into production. Modern agricultural techniques such as better varieties, better animal breeding practises, better feeding and cropping techniques, even supplemental water for a few dry summer weeks in normally humid farming areas, will make possible increased agricultural production at costs infinitely lower than those involved in the importation of water to arid regions.

Let us assume, then, that water is being priced in accordance with the real costs of delivering it to the user, and is therefore being used reasonably efficiently. Let us assume further that the objectives for which water development is being suggested, have been carefully assessed and that additional water supplies are likely to be beneficial. We are still far from that point at which the importation of water is a logical step. It is necessary to examine with much more care the use being made of the water available locally.

The first aspect of this question to be considered is that of water quality. Any shortage of water in the United States, or in Canada, is primarily one of *clean* water, and that the promotion of water importation reflects a desire not only for cheap water, as we have seen, but for clean, unpolluted water. It is however obvious that a large quantity of water available to any area is its own waste water. As P. H. McGauhey of the University of California says: "Long before political and engineering arrangements can possibly be made to bring water from Canada, or even from long distances within the United States, the need to make use of local supplies regardless of their present quality will become acute."

Near San Diego in Southern California is a community which has developed a system showing just how practical it can be to make intelligent use of waste water. Santee gets its water from the Colorado River, and pays the Metropolitan Water District of Southern California $45 per acre foot for it. A few years ago, when faced with a need to expand its sewage disposal system, it decided against joining with San Diego in piping its sewage out to sea. Instead, it set out on an untried course of making use of the water most readily available to it. It decided to make use of its own sewage to reduce its growing requirements for Colorado River water, to provide recreational facilities for the dry valley in which it is located, and to save on the cost of transportating its wastes to sea.

A remarkable system now exists in Santee that attracts visitors from all over the world. After primary, secondary, and tertiary treatment, the water makes its way through 5 small lakes. Where once sagebrush grew, more than three hundred thousand people a year boat, swim and fish in the beautiful tree-shaded lakes formed from the waste water which might have been more pollution added to the ocean. The overflow water is used to irrigate a golf course, a tree nursery and parks, and a pilot system is being worked out to provide an auxiliary water system for private homes which will use the water for lawns and gardens. Another project produces 100,000 gallons per day of drinking water from the waste water, but it is not yet economical to treat large volumes of water for recycling into the drinking water system. As technology in this field continues its very rapid advances, and as it becomes increasingly expensive to bring in water from far away, total recycling will at some point become economical, Santee authorities are sure. Of one thing they are convinced — the psychological barrier to such use is not an important factor, since the use of reclaimed sewage water for recreational purposes was accepted enthusiastically from the beginning.

The Santee project is important to Canadians for two reasons. It shows that much better use can be made of water in many areas of the United States that are pleading water shortages, and from which pressure is growing for importation of Canadian water. Existing surface and ground water supplies in such regions can be greatly "stretched" using such systems, and Canadians should not consider genuine any claim of need unless such techniques are in use. Then too, the Santee system, or adaptations of parts of it, could be examined for application in those areas of Canada which are concerned about the double-barrelled problem of water supply and sewage disposal. The Okanagan Valley and parts of the southern prairies are obvious examples where such programs might be studied at greater profit than continuing the perennial claim by some that water diversion into these regions is required. As McGauhey puts it: "The importation of water to make it possible to continue present wasteful practises is senseless and untenable from any resource conservation viewpoint."

At the University of Arizona at Tucson, research is proceeding along a number of lines designed to develop better use of water resources in areas presumed to have shortages. With respect to waste water treatment Dr. Sol Resnick states that "sewage effluent exceeds 50% of the total water consumption of municipalities in Arizona. Hence a sizeable amount of water exists . . . that with proper treatment can be made available for even domestic use at prices less than that for water brought in by means of large-scale transfers." Tucson is experimenting with a project similar to that at Santee, expecting it to be an important part of the solution to both water supply and pollution control. At the university, research proceeds into the best means of returning industrial cooling water, or treated waste water, into the underground aquifers which supply so much of the water of the Southwest. This is being done on a practical scale in the Los Angeles area at Whittier Narrows. Flood waters and treated waste water is spread over areas of permeable material such as sand and gravel and it percolates down into nature's underground reservoirs. Similar results are being achieved though the use of injection wells and recharge shafts.

As indicated earlier, evaporation is a serious problem in arid areas, and several approaches to this are being tried at the University of Arizona. Shore-mounted dispensers meter long-chain alcohol onto the surface of a reservoir to spread out into a film one molecule in thickness. This very thin layer reduces evaporation by 30 per cent. A pound of alcohol covers 20 acres of water, but so far the process has not been economical as it costs about $1000 for each acre foot of water saved. One problem is dispersal by the wind, but even so it is thought that larger scale applications than have so far been tried would bring substantially lower costs.

A more promising idea has been the spreading of great numbers of floating styrofoam or cement rafts on reservoirs; this is reducing evaporation at a cost of about $65 per acre foot of water saved. This is comparable to the cost of large scale water transfers. Such a technique would however reduce the value of a reservoir for recreational purposes.

Several methods are being tried to capture the water that naturally occurs in dry regions. 80 million acre-feet of water rains on Arizona annually, for example, and only 4 or 5 per cent of it is captured and used. For small scale use by municipalities and farms, polyethylene sheeting on hillsides, covered with fine gravel, is showing promise. For large scale "water harvesting" it has been found that the spreading of common salt on desert watersheds seals the surface and causes the water to runoff from rainstorms in a way that makes its capture possible. Though much remains to be worked out in this method, it appears that it may provide water at prices attractive for irrigation use.

Watershed management is a vital aspect of water conservation in humid areas as well as arid ones. The Saskatchewan River and its tributaries are the most important sources of water in Alberta and Saskatchewan. The Saskatchewan is a vital factor in Manitoba's water balance too. Almost all of its flow originates in the eastern Rocky Mountains of Alberta, and to ensure that the water conserving qualities of the area were respected, the Eastern Rockies Forest Conservation Board was established in 1947 to administer the 9000 square miles of watershed lying outside the National Parks. Although water conservation is established as the prime function of the area, there are fears that overgrazing of cattle, overcutting of timber, road building, seismic lines for oil and gas exploration, and mining exploration, may be gradually reducing the water yield of the eastern Rockies.

Strip mining of coal in the past has been catastrophic to quality of water in streams. The revival of coal mining in the Rocky Mountains in its vast new stripmining format is showing destructive effects on streams in southeastern British Columbia already, and such developments in the eastern Rockies of Alberta could have implications for water quality throughout the prairie provinces. The author has seen Alberta Highway Department bulldozers obliterate a fine mountain stream as they pushed their blades back and forth through it in the interests of some minor road repair. Such activities reflect an attitude that could bode ill for the watershed of the eastern Rockies.

Proper watershed management is a vital factor in maintaining relatively even flows of water, and in maintaining a quality supply of water. Properly maintained trees and vegetation of all kinds are more effective than the great dams that are often built to replace destroyed watersheds. Flooding and drought are the companion of damaged watersheds, as has been proven in the redwood forests of California and the sad lands of strip-mined Kentucky and West Virginia, and by the flood-ravaged art treasures of Florence.

Other factors are reducing the water-regulating function performed so well by nature. Swamplands act as great sponges, as well as being enormously productive in a biological sense. They soak up water when lots of it is available, slowly releasing it later into the streams and rivers. When these wet land are drained or filled in, runoff is faster and may increase sufficiently to bring forth a demand for flood control dams. Similarly, the spread of suburban development over watersheds eliminates the natural absorpitive capacity of landscape, and the fast runoff from roofs and streets contributes to flash flooding at some times, and dried up streams at others.

Desalinization of sea water has long been suggested as a way of ultimately solving the problem of water shortages in arid areas. The Metropolitan Water District of Southern California very nearly proceeded with a combined nuclear power plant and desalting facility on a man-made island near Los Angeles, before escalating cost rules the project out. In Mexico a critical shortage of drinking water existed at the city of Tijuana, just south of the U.S. border. Between 1950 and 1970 the population multiplied five times, from 60,000 to 330,000. The problems accompanying this growth were enormous in almost every respect, but particularly so in the case of water. When a drought hit the region at the same time, the situation became critical. Many people got only enough water to sustain life. Ground water resources were depleted and costs of bringing water by aqueduct across the desert from the Colorado River were prohibitive, particularly in view of the high rate of interest that would have to be paid for the money required to buildit. And, it should be noted, use and manipulation of the Colorado River in the U.S. results in water that is almost unusable by the time it reaches Mexico anyway.

And so Tijuana built the continent's largest desalting plant in association with an oil-fired electric power plant at Rosarita Beach, a few miles south of the city. It supplies water at a cost of 65 cents per thousand gallons, or $212 per acre foot. Expensive, but it appeared to be the only way of providing for the needs of Tijuana.

Opinions vary as to the future of large scale use of desalted sea water for man's use. Economist Kenneth Boulding says: "Desalinization is a will-of-the-wisp. Let's face it. It is nonsense. The energy requirements are enormous; the transport costs are enormous. The whole trouble with oceans is that they are terribly low. It is all right for Kuwait, it is all right for high industrial purposes. But this idea of desalinization giving us unlimited quantities of water everywhere in the world is bunk." Conversely, Canada's Environment Minister Jack Davis suggested in June of 1970 that unless Canada sold water to the United States soon, desalinization would be supplying all the water the Americans needed and Canada would have lost a market for her water.

As far as the economics of desalting are concerned, Boulding has probably put his finger on it. The costs of lifting water and pumping it inland over large distances are very great, and will probably limit the technique to use close to the oceans. But that still leaves a great deal of room for this technology. California, the most populous state in the U.S., amasses the bulk of its population along the coast. A. D. K. Laird of the University of California at Berkeley is a leading authority in the field, and he states that water could be produced now by a big plant using the latest technology at a cost of $68 per acre foot. This is about what large scale water transfers are expected to cost, and while it is far beyond the price that could be paid for use of water in irrigated agriculture, it is a reasonable price for industrial and municipal use. Laird expects this cost to come down further, and predicts that by early in the next century, "desalted water will be cheaper than other means of water supply augmentation." There remain of course many problems — the most obvious is perhaps the disposal of the enormous amounts of salt that would be created by such plants, or more likely the returning to the sea of the concentrated brine that would remain when fresh water was drawn off. The effect of this on the marine ecology of areas affected is as yet unknown.

There are interesting variations on this theme. Salty water is found underground in many locations, and though it is not drinkable it contains far less salt in most instances than does sea water. And so at considerably less cost, this brackish water can be made potable. This has been done to supply water for the town of Buckeye, Arizona.

Then there is a fascinating project at the University of Arizona which involves the production of power, water, and food in a single co-ordinated system. The oceans of the world have some 20,000 miles of desert coastline, and it is in such regions that the researchers see their ideas being applied. At Puerto Penasco in Mexico on the Gulf of California, a pilot plant built in co-operation with the University of Sonora generates electricity, distills sea water, and grows food. The power is produced by diesel generators, which ordinarily dissipate two-thirds of their energy into the air as waste heat. Here, however, it is used to distill sea water, which in turn is used for the growing of lettuce, tomatoes, peppers, strawberries, melons, and many other vegetables. The secret is in the use of inflated greenhouses made of polyethelene which keeps the water virtually in a closed circuit system. Desalted sea water is far too expensive for use in ordinary open-air agriculture, but this system uses only one tenth as much water, since the plastic greenhouse prevents it from evaporating. The water is recycled again and again through the system. Carbon dioxide seems to encourage plant growth, and research proceeds to use that product of the diesel generators in the greenhouses as well, making the system even more enclosed and productive. The first commercial installation of the system is being prepared for the desert sheikdom of Abu Dhabi, on the Arabian Peninsula.

Although there are a great many physical alternatives to the actual transfer of large quantities of water, some of them pose real difficulties and may cause problems more serious than those they are supposed to solve. Under certain conditions, watersheds with fewer trees yield more total water than heavily forested slopes, since the trees use and transpire into the atmosphere some of the water which falls on them. It was perhaps inevitable that someone would suggest removing the tree growth on the higher lands of northern Arizona to increase the water yield of the region for the benefit of the southern desert areas. We are familiar with the results of this sort of watershed treatment.

Along the same lines, an active program for control of "phreatophytes" (water-loving plants) has been followed along some Arizona rivers. This means the denuding of river banks, the only place where plants grow extensively in many desert areas. Conservationists and scientists in Arizona have vigorously protested the program, since it removes the habitat of wildlife, and according to ecologist Dr. Gerald Cole of Arizona State University, more than 90 per cent of fish have been eliminated in some stretches of streams where the banks have been cleared. He insists that such programs result in increased erosion of river banks, covering spawning beds and adding to siltation of reservoirs. The watercourses are no longer shaded by trees, and increased evaporation is inevitable, he points out.

Another practise eliminating the natural aspect of the rivers of the desert is one called "channelization," in which rivers are straightened and deepened, again in the hope that by totally engineering them, a greater water yield will result. Alarm about the consequences of this operation has also been expressed by conservation and scientific groups.

Then there is the question of weather modification. In an arid area, this means rain-making. The subject has been under serious study for some years, particularly at the U.S. National Centre for Atmospheric Research at Boulder, Colorado. Even if the scientific difficulties in controlling rainfall were solved, there remain monumental legal, moral, economic, and social and environmental problems. If you make it rain in one place, it will rain less somewhere else possibly with serious consequences for all forms of life and activity. If you make it rain today to benefit the crops, the sponsors of a tourist festival may sue you. As this book goes to press, there seems a possibility that the U.S. Bureau of Reclamation was experimenting with weather modification at the time and in the area of the torrential downpours that breached a dam and caused great loss of life in South Dakota in July 1972. If this is established, it seems inevitable that lawsuits will be mounted to extract damages from the Bureau, and the amounts involved would probably be astronomical.

But there are almost endless sound alternatives to conventional water development. Flood control is a prime reason for many water projects, yet as we noted in chapter 6, there are many other ways of dealing with such a threat. Historically, flood control dams have often resulted in increased damage in the area supposedly protected, yet such technological solutions have drawn attention away from more genuine solutions to the problem, such as watershed protection or rehabilitation, flood plain zoning, flood insurance, diking, and floodproofing.

We have seen that technology exists that will greatly reduce the requirements for water by agricultural, industrial, and municipal users, and that there are economic and institutional measures that would bring this about are obvious. Additionally, many of the water supply problems of the United States could be solved simply by sorting out the legal problems relating to water. The whole field is so confused that some advocates of water export, such as Dr. Arleigh Laycock of the University of Alberta, have suggested that Canada could supply water to the U.S. to save them the trouble of sorting out their laws. Clearly, however, some effort in the court rooms and legislatures of the United States would be a preferable solution to the manipulation of the rivers of both countries. The employment provided in the legal profession alone might make it worthwhile!

Ludicrous laws which reach far back in time often result in water users in the U.S. taking more than they need to preserve their rights to the water. There are laws which make it very difficult to transfer water from low value uses to those of higher value, and in many areas there are no laws to promote the conservation of declining water tables. Many of the traditions that were perhaps reasonable in a pioneering, underpopulated nation have become enshrined in law, making it difficult to apply new thinking and new policies to a land that may well be over-populated and in many areas is certainly over-developed. To expect other parts of the United States, and to expect Canada, to come to the aid of areas which have not made the effort necessary to straighten out the legal and institutional absurdities that prevent rational water policies, is surely unacceptable.

For when all the economic, institutional, and physical alternatives to great water developments have been considered and applied where possible, whether for water supply or for energy, there will still be pressures for the manipulation of our water resources on a grand scale if present trends continue. This brings us face to face with the real alternative to endless "development", whether of water or of other resources. Recognition that the world and its resources provide a finite home for man and the other members of the biosphere; that there are limits to the growth that can occur in a given space; and that exhaustion of some resources and destruction of most of them is a very real possibility is difficult for a society whose institutions are largely based upon an assumption that endless growth is possible and desirable. Recognition of constraints within which man must live is foreign to the thinking of many North Americans, yet clearly we must sooner or later face the realities of a "spaceship earth", as the concept has been termed by economists Kennth Boulding and Barbara Ward.

The real question is *when*, not *whether*, we will have to recognize the limits of our earth, and in this case of the water resources of this continent. We have seen that there are almost endless possibilities for making better use of water while recognizing that development must be limited to available supplies, efficiently used. We might, with economist James A. Crutchfield, suggest: "Maybe Arizona is supposed to be dry." And we could say the same of Manitoba's Souris River Valley, or we could recognize that the Great Lakes operate pretty well and don't really need the water that presently flows into James Bay.

Alternatively, we can restructure the natural water systems of the continent, whether in great international water diversion schemes or in manipulations within the borders of our countries, until once again we come up against the limits imposed by a lack of further water supplies to move about. But our requirements will at that time be growing at a faster rate than ever. It is clear from our discussion that the price we will have paid in environmental damage, social disruption, and economic chaos will by then be extreme, and it will be a sadly demeaned world with which we will have to come to terms.

Chapter 9

Water policy for Canada: where do we go from here?

There exists in Canada no effective policy regarding the care and use of the nation's water resources. There are on record thousands of words of speeches, statements, guidelines, and declarations of good intentions of many kinds. These have been made by federal and provincial cabinet ministers, and various officials of both levels of government. All this fine phraseology shares the unique characteristic of having nothing whatever to do with the way in which water development has occurred in Canada, or the way in which plans and programs for water development are proceeding in Canada at the present time. The intent of this chapter is to show some of the consequences that have been inherent in this lack of a coherent water policy, and to indicate a few of the principles which should be basic in developing such a policy.

Some of the earlier water developments were probably appropriate for their time. The era of much larger projects which began in the nineteen fifties has for the most part proceeded without modification of the principles that may once have been valid but which make no recognition of the changing nature of the country and its requirements, or of the people and their values. Water development decision-making in Canada proceeds largely in a manner innocent of modern water management principles, yet employs the latest engineering techniques which make possible projects of a scale (and often destructiveness) impossible earlier in the century.

Dams and diversions in Canada have often been the product of political grandstand plays, a latter day equivalent of Roman circuses presented to convince the citizens that their governments are accomplishing magnificent things on their behalf. Water development in Canada since World War Two has often been remarkable for its lack of relationship to economic reality, and its lack of consideration for environmental factors. Furthermore, Canadian water development has been characterized by almost no involvement of the people of Canada, and in fact an atmosphere of secrecy is normal in such programs. Altogether, it is a strange way to proceed with the irrevocable manipulation of the most precious resource belonging to the people of Canada.

Harsh words, perhaps. The basis for them has been in large measure the content of this book. Consider the Columbia River Treaty and its dams, the Big Horn Dam in Alberta, the Gardiner Dam on the South Saskatchewan River, the Mactaquac Dam on New Brunswick's Saint John River, Newfoundland's Bay D'Espoir project. Consider those projects just getting under way, which carry the shortcomings of the above projects to even greater lengths — the diversion of the Churchill River to the Nelson River in Manitoba, for instance, and the James Bay project in Quebec. Consider the multiple project schemes that to date are lines on a map or in some cases elaborate computer printouts: The Saskatchewan-Nelson Basin Study, Alberta's PRIME program, the Northern Ontario diversion studies, for example. These latter programs, involving the two senior levels of government in Canada, differ little in philosophy from that represented by the ultimate lunacy of the great continental water schemes such as NAWAPA, the Smith Plan, CeNAWAP and many others.

But the men who have promoted water developments of this kind are not generally malicious people, and even where projects have been undertaken largely for political advantage it is likely that there has not been an understanding of the consequences of the decision. Our water resources, as we have seen, have probably been more completely misunderstood and surrounded by mythical concepts than any other resource. Then too, economic assessments of water developments have been so unsophisticated and so misleading that some of the horrendous choices of the past can be understood.

None of this, of course, excuses what is now occurring in the field of water development in Canada. The lessons of the past should be abundantly clear, and modern water management principles should long since have been accepted and applied throughout the country. What seems to have happened is that water resource planners in the lower echelons of government, particularly the federal government, have in fact been proposing and fighting for more enlightened policies and programs, but these have had little or no impact at the decision-making level. Conferences and seminars amongst government and University water experts abound, and esoteric aspects of water management are dissected in minute detail. But it all goes on at a level totally isolated from reality. While the experts discuss planning and economic and environmental aspects of rivers and lakes, politicians and hydro authorities are busily manipulating the water resources of the nation in response to quite different imperatives.

When it is no longer possible totally to reject studies that could lead to modern water planning procedures, the pattern in Canada is to allow such studies to proceed, with the explicit or implicit provision that the results will not be allowed to influence what actually occurs. For example, the federal-provincial studies currently underway on the environmental aspects of the Churchill-Nelson scheme of Manitoba Hydro at a cost of two million dollars was approved by Manitoba officials only after assurances were included in the study agreement that the results would not affect the decisions already taken to proceed with the projects. The agreement states:

Certain information will be taken as given, namely that Lake Winnipeg will be regulated between the levels of 711 and 715 feet elevation and that Southern Indian Lake will be raised to not more than 850 feet elevation for a diversion out of the Churchill River of up to 30,000 cubic feet per second.

These are the developments that the study is all about, of course; and so with one sentence the entire two million dollar study is reduced to farcical proportions. The striking thing about this agreement is that this clause was insisted upon by the Manitoba Government of Premier Edward Schreyer, which in part owed its election to a promise carefully to re-examine the entire Churchill-Nelson project. A re-examination will occur, but it will have nothing to do with the decision itself. It has already been made. The only change from the proposals of the previous government is that Southern Indian Lake will not be flooded as deeply — but according to Dr. Robert Newbury of the University of Manitoba, one of the people most knowledgeable about the water resources of the region, 75 per cent of the damage will occur even at the lower level of flooding.

A preliminary study of the possible environmental impact of the huge James Bay project in Quebec carried out by another federal-provincial task force reported in December of 1971:

It is understood that the decision to proceed has been taken. This report therefore does not reflect any personal or collective reservations held by the Task Force members as to whether the society really needs the project, whether there are more economical and less environmentally disturbing ways of harnessing energy resources to meet Quebec's future electric power requirements, or whether society should strive to restrain its electrical demands rather than increase its supply. It was assumed that these fundamental questions had been adequately considered by the authorities prior to making their decision to proceed.

In fact, of course, there is no evidence whatever that any of these questions have been given consideration by the government of Quebec. The two studies carried out by consulting engineering firms and upon which the decision appears to have been based, do not mention social or ecological factors even in passing.

It is very clear that most of Canada's Water resource decision makers are continuing to operate on the presumption that growth - and - technology - at - whatever - cost is still the unquestioned goal of this country. There is much evidence that this simply is no longer true, that most of the old assumptions are being questioned if not discarded, and that the expectations and requirements of the people of Canada are broadening rapidly to include insistence on a quality environment and an opportunity for diversity of choice in life styles. None of this is yet influencing water policy in this country, although as we have noted it is being recognized in public speeches. Obviously, then, a way must be found to reflect the needs and aspirations of our people in our water policy.

Lack of knowledge on the part of the public is the largest single barrier to public participation in the decision making process. There are a number of reasons for this. One of course is that many of our greatest water resources are distant from centres of population, and so Canadians just do not know what they have, and what they are losing in large scale water development. Overcoming this fact of geography is in itself a challenge of considerable proportions, but it is made much more difficult by a dominant feature of water development in Canada: secrecy.

From coast to coast, water development has been characterized by a cloak and dagger atmosphere that makes open debate of the issues involved impossible. In most provinces, every effort is made to keep water planning under wraps until final and often irrevocable decisions have been made; then a grand announcement is made with all the appropriate flourishes. The work is under way before the public really knows what is happening.

Examples are to be found almost everywhere. Alberta conservationists insist that the bulldozers were already at work on the Big Horn Dam reservoir before anyone knew what was happening. At that stage the issue was forced into a legislative hearing, but there was no turning back the flooding of the beautiful and historic valley. In Ontario, the federal-provincial studies of dams and diversions throughout the northern part of the province have been kept extremely quiet, with conflicting statements as to their purpose being issued from time to time. The anger of the people of the area deepened with the cavalier treatment given by authorities of both levels of governments to their requests for information.

In British Columbia, a Vancouver *Sun* editor stumbled upon major dam site surveys being carried out on the Stikine and Iskut Rivers by the British Newfoundland Corporation, but provincial government authorities insisted they knew nothing about it. It was later revealed that a provincial cabinet minister had visited the area with the American Ambassador, but still no one would speak. In the meantime, BRINCO was telling Newfoundlanders that it was choosing between Newfoundland and British Columbia as a site for the power generation facilities to operate a uranium enrichment plant. This process requires enormous amounts of power to create the fuel used in the American type of nuclear power plant, and since still nothing was being said by government authorities, the visit of the U.S. Ambassador to the area took on obvious connotations. Everybody but British Columbians, it seems, could be told and consulted about the possible disposition of another great salmon river and water resource belonging to the people of the province.

A major study by the B.C. Energy Board, which was to recommend the manner in which the province should meet its energy requirements projected for 1985, is a classic of its kind. Committees, composed of leading experts in many aspects of water development, were established to advise the Board. Upon appointment, these consultants were told that all aspects of the study were to be secret. Similar orders were given to all the professionals within B.C. Hydro and its engineering subsidiary, IPEC. In one step, therefore, the public had its most knowledgeable potential critics removed from any possibility of public debate on the matter. Location studies of the Board were carried on in an almost clandestine manner, with field parties refusing to acknowledge the purpose of their geological and engineering surveys. Committee reports that described serious problems of an environmental nature that would arise with the construction of favoured projects, were sent back for re-writing and softening.

Perhaps most serious of all is the fact that the Energy Board had been assigned to recommend methods of generating power in amounts that were arrived at by studies which amounted to little more than an extrapolation of the current growth rates of power consumption in the province. That increase is occurring much faster than population is growing, due in no small part to the vigorous promotion of electrical consumption by B.C. Hydro. The fundamental questions as to whether or not the people of the province wish this type of growth to continue, whether a highly industrialized future is likely to provide the best life for the people of the province, or whether other less damaging sources of energy than those currently in use might be considered, were not asked or discussed. All of this was accepted as being "given", and the people of the province were allowed no comment on the future they will be required to pay for.

In Manitoba, Hydro and Government were so anxious to avoid the open hearings that had been provided for in establishing the Manitoba Water Commission, that it pressured the Commission into merely holding public information meetings on the question of the regulation of Lake Winnipeg for greater power generation on the Nelson River. The board was therefore unable to hold formal hearings, call and cross-examine witnesses, or make recommendations on its findings.

Such an emasculation of the Commission, which the previous government had established as a body independent of the Government and reporting directly to the Legislature, precipitated the resignation of one of Manitoba's most knowledgeable and enlightened water resource experts, Dr. Robert Newbury of the University of Manitoba. Dr. Newbury in his resignation regretted that the Commission had been able to spend very little time examining the most important water issues in the province — the regulation of Lake Winnipeg and the diversion of the Churchill River into the Nelson River for the maximization of power generation:

These are issues which will profoundly affect the landscape and use of Manitoba for all times and as such deserve the fullest possible investigation and public review. The irreversible value judgments now being made are so fundamental to the future character of Manitoba that I believe their assessment should be above party politics and the machinations of departments and Crown Corporations.
Preliminary evidence suggests that we are imposing a severe strain on the natural environment of our two largest rivers and lakes in order to achieve unspecified hydro-electric benefits. As these are largely the remaining water resources that are not committed to development, the mode and skill of their development deserve the particular concern of an independent commission and an informed public.
I see no evidence of this happening.

Other members of the Manitoba Water Commission, including its highly respected chairman, Professor Cass Booy, stayed on, hoping that it would still be possible to accomplish something useful. It was evident however that properly constituted hearings would be necessary to adequately examine Hydro's plans for Lake Winnipeg and Southern Indian Lake, and when Professor Booy and Commission member Mike Kawchuk insisted on this, they were removed from office. A new chairman was appointed who has no background in water resource matters.

Premier Schreyer is now assured of a quiescent Manitoba Water Commission, and a promising innovation that would have kept the people of Manitoba informed about the use or abuse of their water resources, has become a vanished dream. The first real attempt in Canada to break away from the secrecy typical of water resource development has come to an end.

The situation is even more blatant in Quebec, where the pretense of a second look, as occurred in Manitoba, has not taken place. A decision which was announced as final was sprung on the people of the province with all the hoopla of a Ringling Brothers opening day. The environmental, social and economic implications of this project we have looked at elsewhere, but as in most other cases in Canada, these were not brought to light by those to whom the care of the nation's resources have been entrusted. The pattern was little different in the damming of the Saint John River in New Brunswick by the Mactaquac Dam, or the Bay D'Espoir power project in Newfoundland, which drowned hundreds of square miles of wilderness to provide subsidized power for the Electric Reduction Company on Placentia Bay.

The muzzling of those people most expert in water resource development is a serious hindrance to any kind of democratic consideration of public issues. "The Silenced Minority" these people might be called, and yet they are paid from the public purse, have been educated largely at public expense, and many of them are employed in public institutions. It is demanded of them that their commitment be to the officials and politicians senior to them, rather than to the people of Canada. Their efforts must be focussed on seeing that "The Plan" is realized, rather than providing the knowledge, expertise and advice that would enable the public to make better choices. Throughout government of both levels, files and documents are marked "confidential" until long after they could be of any value to the public in understanding the true issues involved.

So water development in Canada does not present an admirable picture for anyone who believes in the right of the people to know, or to any population who believes that democracy means open government. It should surely not be necessary for the people of Canada to fear what their governments are doing with their resources, and indeed with the future of their country, behind closed doors.

The first and most fundamental aspect of a Canadian water policy, then, must be complete openness and deliberate involvement of the people of the country in the choices that must be made. This does not mean simply holding hearings on a "grand plan" that has been threshed out in private and presented as the single best way of proceeding. That provides no choice at all. Those proposing water development must first demonstrate that the project is essential for some social purpose. The movement of water or the generation of energy is not a goal in itself, although it often is treated as such in Canada. The goal for which the development is proposed must be subject to public scrutiny, whether it be to provide water for irrigation, for industrial or municipal purposes, to provide for flood control, or navigation on a river, or to generate electricity for domestic purposes or for export to the United States.

Whatever the goal, it must be clearly spelled out and agreed upon in public. If the goal is a valid one, then water development must be considered along with a whole range of alternative ways of achieving it. We have touched upon the question of hydro development for electrical generation, and it seems clear that a great many questions need to be answered before a project for this purpose proceeds. Is the best use being made of power currently available? Is the requirement for a dam simply to satisfy a demand that is in fact being created by the agency wishing to build the facility? Will the industrialization that may be fueled by the projected facility add or detract from the way of life desired by the people of the area involved? And if the answer is affirmative, and indeed more electrical energy is required, is damming a river the best way of achieving it? Have conventional alternatives such as oil, gas, or coal fired plants been carefully assessed for their relative advantages and disadvantages, has nuclear power been considered? All such sources have apparent disadvantages and so for longer range solutions are we as a society putting emphasis on research to achieve better means of energy production? Are we adequately investigating solar or fusion power, for instance?

In the case of irrigation, we have seen that in the United States intensive irrigation development was initiated for a social purpose: the establishment of familites on the lands of the western states. Irrigation farming in those areas has long since passed into the hands of huge industrialized agribusiness, yet the water organizations continue to build facilities to accomplish totally different goals than those for which they were established. Similarly in Canada, the large early irrigation projects in Alberta were designed to provide business for the Canadian Pacific Railway. Somewhere along the way, irrigation became accepted as a goal in itself, and was held as an end worth pursuing at whatever cost. And so the Gardiner Dam on the South Saskatchewan River was built at enormous cost to provide irrigated land for products that were not required, displacing the dry land farmers of the area that had no interest whatever in irrigation farming.

If it is suggested that water is required for municipal purposes, we must ask if adequate metering and pricing of present supplies is ensuring that the water available is being used with reasonable care. Similarly, if industrial uses are involved, we must ask if industries presently in the area are making the much more intensive use of the resource through recycling and other means that are readily applicable in most cases. If the desire, through water diversion or power generation is to encourage industry into an area we must ask if such industry will in fact be attracted, since ample water and energy has failed to be a talisman in so many other regions. And if they can be attracted, are these the industries that will employ people in sufficient numbers to make up for the inevitable problems such as pollution, disruption of land use patterns, and other factors that accompany industrialization. If water consuming industry is being encouraged in the hope of adding to the economic growth of the area, is this in fact the most desirable way of achieving that end? It is possible that the money would better aid the economy through, perhaps, improved educational facilities, or improved transportation? It should be remembered that the very industries attracted to an area into which water has been diverted would probably be those least desirable. High water consuming businesses make least sense where imported water is used, since such water is inevitably higher in real cost than it would be where natural supplies occur in abundance. Industry that relies very little on water, or that capitalizes on the natural assets of the region, such as tourism, makes much more sense in an area that does not naturally have a great amount of water.

Dr. Derrick Sewell of the University of Victoria suggests: "I think ultimately people in Canada will begin to place much higher values on their resources and particularly their water resources. In British Columbia, for example, this province could eventually become a playground for North America and, if that is to be the case, I think that the preservation of our water resources would be to our advantage. This is probably true in other parts of Canada too. With higher incomes and more leisure time; with greater access to different parts of our country we must provide the opportunities, and water based recreation probably will be one of the most valuable in the future."

The alternatives to massive water development are almost without number, as we have seen. Ways in which to approach them have been put forth clearly in much of the best water resources literature of recent years. Water development agencies, however, have generally stated the needs for water or energy as imperatives, as needs that not only must be achieved, but that must be achieved very quickly, and that no other way of approaching the situation will suffice. In fact, however, as the authoritative text *Water Supply* states: "There are few fixed requirements for water." Or as resource economist Guner Schramm puts it: "Water is about the most easily substitutable natural resource input to almost any type of human activity that exists." Conversely, it is the indispensible resource required for the maintenance of the health of the land of which it is a part.

All of these questions and alternatives, and many more besides, must be explored not only in the region where water development is proposed, but also where the diverted water or the generated energy is to be used. For example, the Colorado River states of the U.S. comprise an area where importation of Canadian water is considered by many to be inevitable. Yet the prestigious Committee on Water established by the National Academy of Sciences in the United States states: "Relatively few of the alternative means of achieving various aims of water management in the Colorado basin have been considered adequately. Planning has centered largely on manipulation of the water resource itself, and other ways of realizing objectives have been neglected."

Water agencies and governments frequently suggest a great urgency for water developments of various kinds. It is often said that some great project is required by a certain target date, with dire consequences for society if this goal is not achieved. The urgency of the project is such that there is insufficient time for adequate citizen participation in the decision making process. Such reasoning is clearly specious, and should be totally rejected. That the disruption of great water systems for all time must be rushed ahead in answer to someone's paper projections, and that this is sufficient reason for excluding the people of Canada from participation in the future of their country, is intolerable — particularly since the citizens will be required to pay for it. Yet this is a very common state of affairs in Canada. We should note too that the projections of needs and costs upon which such urgency is based are frequently grossly inaccurate, or at least are in the nature of a "self-fulfilling prophecy".

An extremely useful part of public involvement would be a continuing public accounting of all water development projects. The actual realized costs of water projects, in economic, social and biological terms, published along with the pre-construction estimates of these costs and benefits, would be enlightening information and would provide a basis upon which to accept or discount the projections of various agencies as they promote new projects. Such accounting, like the responsibility for public involvement through hearings and other mechanisms, should be the province of agencies separate from those proposing and building water and power facilities. It is interesting to note that in both the United States and Canada it is difficult to obtain the real costs and benefits of projects once they are completed. The agencies concerned are usually compiling lists of benefits and costs for the next project without really knowing how accurate they were on the last one. Nor are they particularly anxious to find out, in many cases; Garrett Hardin has pointed out that "planners who make errors are likely deliberately to interfere with the free flow of information in order to save their skins."

We are a long way from understanding the best ways of achieving genuine public involvement; but then of course we haven't tried very hard to find it. The kind of effort that goes into keeping water development decision making secret would go a long way toward finding a way of adequately involving the public. Certainly, the public hearing, conducted by impartial agencies with full power to call and examine witnesses, is a vital part of the process. Long before this, however, people should be a part of the planning, and the federal-provincial studies presently occurring in the Okanagan, Qu'Appelle, and Saint John River Valleys include tentative attempts at finding new and more effective ways of involving the public. It must be recognized, however that "public involvement" can be a euphemism for public propagandizing, occurring as it often does after decisions have essentially been made. This was the case for example in the "public information meetings" held in Manitoba in 1972 regarding the regulation of Lake Winnipeg by Manitoba Hydro. "Public involvement" may also be farcical if key elements relating to eventual decisions are not subject to discussion. For instance, the current federal - provincial Okanagan Basin study accepts economic growth as a basic policy for the valley, yet whether or not extensive growth should be encouraged is a contentious issue amongst residents of the valley.

The key point is: if the full range of social decisions and the value judgements implicit in water development are not laid out before the public as properly developed alternatives, then the agency responsible has in fact reserved such decisions for itself, and has far overstepped its rights as a technical agency. Any plan or project set forth as the single best solutions to any problems, must be viewed in this light.

Many difficult aspects of water policy are more easily resolved with the recognition that Canada's free-flowing water is a vital part of her existence as a nation, a thesis that will be developed in the next chapter. For instance, the study of our water resources would be continued and increased, but the emphasis changed to stress our need to understand more clearly the complexity of these intricate living systems and their relationships to human needs. This contrasts with the nature of most Canadian water studies to date which are designed to identify ways in which rivers can be dammed, diverted, or in some way manipulated. The deeper understanding of our water resources derived from such a change in emphasis would provide the basis for a Canadian water policy that would have as its cornerstone the need to learn how to live *with* the water resources of the country.

Such a policy would be designed to help Canadians make optimum use of the nation's waters *where they are*, and with minimum disturbance to their functioning as natural systems. Our water resource location and flow would largely be regarded as "given" in the same sense as the hours of sunshine in an area are a natural phenomenon, or that the temperatures of a region will determine what crops can be grown there; or that the topography of an area is a characteristic that is accepted and lived with.

This is not at all a primitive approach that would prevent development in Canada. On the contrary, there is pragmatic reason enough for such an approach. We know that our natural water systems function well and will serve us perpetually if we allow them to; we know that many dams and diversions are temporary in their benefits, though often permanent in their disruption of life systems. We know that there is always a price to be paid for large-scale water developments in social and environmental losses greatly exceeding those usually predicted. We know that water development time after time has proven an inefficient use of scarce capital needed for other national purposes; we know that the quantity of water available is a far less important factor in regional development that is often suggested by water development promoters, and that proven methods exist to make vastly more efficient use of the water which is naturally available in a region.

Many specific policy guidelines grow naturally out of such a shift in basic attitudes. One of the more important is the need to consider Canadian water development in toto, rather than one project at a time. We should consider the kind of country Canada will be when present and proposed water development programs are completed. With recognition of the importance to the nation of free-flowing rivers, it would be unacceptable to cost each successive water project in the same economic, social and biological way; the damming of the second last wild river in Canada is surely a greater loss to the nation than was the second one. Development continuing on a one-at-a-time basis will persist until there are no wild rivers of consequence remaining. Probably our greatest problem in achieving a total approach is the prevalent attitude that we have so many rivers that development of a few more can make little difference.

Another outcome of an examination of water development in total would be adequate consideration of cumulative effects of water projects. For example, it has been suggested that the James Bay project of Quebec might have an effect upon the climate of parts of Ontario and Quebec. Add to the James Bay project the possible effects of diversions being studied in Northern Ontario, and the change in the water regime of the Nelson, and the drastic reduction of the flow of the Churchill in Manitoba. What changes can be expected in the salinity of Hudson Bay, what additional biological ramifications might be expected that would effect not only weather patterns, but the people, the polar bear, beluga whales, migratory wildfowl and many other forms of life whose existence is quite possibly conditional upon the maintenance of present water regimes? Or is it really more important to provide cheap electricity to New York City and Minneapolis, and perhaps water for Texas?

In the same vein, multi-basin projects such as PRIME, or such as might emerge from the Saskatchewan-Nelson or Northern Ontario studies, should be considered as total systems, not as individual developments linked together. Since as we have seen the first project often triggers a continuing sequence of development, the total effect of all projects in a system should be considered as a consequence of proceeding with the first one.

These are a few of the approaches to policy that might grow out of a recognition that the natural flow of water and the landscape of which it is a vital and creative part is an essential element in the heritage of every Canadian. In its water policy, Canada has an opportunity to re-create a nation that values the natural integrity of its land and water and lives in harmony with them. Such a nation will possess an identity unique on this continent, which will enhance greatly its possibility of independent survival. If however we proceed with the conversion of our great rivers into engineered canals, we will one day realize that the Canada we have idealized no longer exists. Its diversity and beauty and promise will have been submerged by the dams and diversions that have resulted from an attitude that is alien to Canadians. Without her great wild rivers and magnificent silent lakes, there will be much less reason for an independent Canada to exist, and probably much less will to keep it so on the part of her people.

Chapter 10

Water development and the Canadian identity

A myth persists in Canada that ours is an illogical nation. We often think of it as an unlikely stretch of diverse regions divided from their natural north-south relationships by a border arbitrarily fixed on the forty-ninth parallel, along the Great Lakes-St. Lawrence system, and sliced through New England. We credit our existence to those men of the Nineteenth Century who were determined that the northern half of the continent should remain forever British. But it seems unlikely that a nation could share a three thousand mile boundary with a powerful neighbour for more than a century without more fundamental reasons for its birth and survival.

"It is no mere accident that the present Dominion coincides roughly with the fur-trading areas of Northern North America." So wrote one of Canada's greatest historians, Harold A. Innes, in his monumental work, *The Fur Trade In Canada*. The development of the fur-trading economy depended upon large numbers of beaver yielding fur of fine quality, a population of Indians willing and able to trap them, and a transportation network to carry the furs long distances to ocean shipping points on the St. Lawrence River and Hudson Bay. The rivers of Canada provided the highways to market without which the fur trade could not have spread across the continent. Through the economic use of these natural waterways, the men of the North West Company were probably first to recognize the natural unity of the land which became Canada.

The remarkable arrangement of the rivers draining into Hudson Bay and into the St. Lawrence and MacKenzie River basins made it possible to travel east, west, and north across what became Canada. The rims of the river basins are so low that portages connecting them were very short. The canoe, that Indian invention so well adapted to travel on these rivers, could be carried past these minor obstacles. Almost every part of Canada was accessible by canoe. The transcontinental pattern of the fur trade, following the natural water courses of the northern half of continent and based in Montreal, can be seen in the political outline of the Canada of to-day, and many of our commercial institutions share the same roots.

The real accomplishment of the Fathers of Confederation lay in making a political reality of a nation whose form and destiny were the product of its great rivers and the streams and lakes associated with them. It was fitting that one of the main events of Canada's Centennial celebrations in 1967 was a race by canoes representing the ten provinces and two territories from the Rockies to Montreal, following the route of the fur traders. We could celebrate the fact that these historic waterways existed largely unchanged from the days when they were the prime fact in Canada's commercial and political existence.

Within the past decade this situation has begun to change with great rapidity. If the water developments being planned and proposed are carried out, so many dams and diversions will mark our rivers that little will remain of the waterways that created Canada. Some Canadians today would describe the importance of Canada's water in the late twentieth century in terms of horsepower, of acre-feet of water for irrigation, of gallons per day for industrial and domestic use. Some would see it as a commodity for export, like wheat or pulpwood products. But many Canadians would be uncomfortable with such utilitarian views of their country's water. Writes author Roderick Haig-Brown of Campbell River, B.C.: "A river is water in its loveliest form; rivers have life and sound and movement and infinity of variation. Rivers are veins of the earth through which the life blood returns to the heart."

It is likely that most Canadians have given little thought to the water resources of their country, nor have they assessed in a critical way the wide spectrum of existing views about what should be done with them. So it is not easy to determine the meaning of the nation's water resources to Canadians of this generation, and it is even more difficult to formulate an attitude to the water of Canada that will take account of the needs and aspirations of Canadians yet to be born. Because water development is an irreversible process, it surely is essential to try to determine what relationship exists between the water resources of our country, and the nature and identity of Canada and Canadians. We must discover before they have restructured the face of the nation if there is reason to consider the water resources of Canada in terms different from those of water developers and engineers. In the new context of the nineteen-seventies, we must ask if there's a valid reason for trying to re-capture the vision of the men of the North West Company; the concept of a land unified by its free-flowing waters.

For more than two centuries the canoes of the fur brigades plied the waterways of Canada. More than two hundred years of commerce left the rivers virtually unchanged from their original state. Through most of this century, however, we Canadians have viewed our great rivers as resources carrying within them the energy to power a great industrial nation. As Bruce Hutchison wrote in *The Fraser* in 1950: "A river which descends from the Rockies to the coast and spills some 3,000,000,000,000 cubic feet of fresh water into the ocean every year must waste in mere motion an almost unimaginable power. It is not unimaginable to the engineers. They say the Fraser, when harnessed with dams and turbines, can give man 6,000,000 horsepower of electricity. It is probably the largest source of unused power left in the whole of North America. Not long will it remain unused." As he considers the problem of incompatibility of dams and salmon on the Fraser, Hutchison comments, "A government must consider the relative values of various resources. If it has to decide between a million horsepower of electricity, operating a gigantic tidewater industry, and a portion of the salmon run, its choice is obvious." Or as A. E. Paget and C. H. Clay of the B.C. Government stated with reference to the Fraser at the Resources for Tomorrow conference in 1961: ". . . Energy resource values will far outweigh any resource losses consequent to such development."

In her book *The Saskatchewan* Marjorie Campbell reflected the usual Canadian view of the first half of this century. "The annual flow [of the Saskatchewan River] at the Saskatchewan-Manitoba boundary is some 18 million acre-feet, enough water to irrigate hundreds of thousands of acres of dry land and, with that drop of a mile, to generate as much power as Niagara." Reflecting on plans for the total development of the Saskatchewan water system, she says: "The Saskatchewan continues to drain the Rocky Mountains into the Atlantic Ocean. But its flow is no longer wanton, no longer wasted. Or it won't be when the engineers have completed their work, backed by the co-operation of four governments."

168   Water and the Canadian identity

These writers reflected well the attitudes of Canadians as they contemplated the great rewards that could accrue from development of the enormous water resources of the country. "Harnessing" the energy of Churchill Falls in Labrador, Grand Rapids in Manitoba, the Brazeau River in Alberta, was the work of a new and growing Canada, and the men who built the dams and power plants were the giants of the day.

But as some of the potential became realized, doubts began to emerge. Where the Saskatchewan made its last spectacular dash over the limestone rocks of Grand Rapids before losing itself in Lake Winnipeg, Indians and Metis, engineers and politicians, watched as the ancient and historic river died before their eyes on a hot June day in 1964. As the gates of the Grand Rapids dam closed, the flow faltered and faded, and soon all that remained were fish gasping in the pools left among the drying rocks.

A Canadian bank in its 1970 calendar featured a spectacular photograph of Churchill Falls: "Soon to be harnessed . . .". But Canadians are beginning to find that "harnessing" often means "obliterating", that this great spectacle now becomes just one more rocky cliff, the magnificence of its power captured deep underground in humming turbines. It joins the long list of vanished Canadian landmarks — valleys, waterfalls, communities, lakes, rivers, farmlands, wildlife ranges — that have been eradicated from the face of the nation. It was, perhaps, more satisfying to contemplate the possibility of development than to confront the accomplished fact. As mighty dams have risen on the Columbia and the Peace and the Saskatchewan and the Nelson and the Hamilton and the Saint John and many more, and as plans are debated that would dam the Fraser, or divert water from one river to another right across the nation, the dream of "harnessing" and "developing" Canada's water resources is becoming tarnished. Yet, as J. W. MacNeill points out in a study carried out for the Canadian Government, "The St. Lawrence Seaway, the Columbia River project, the Gardiner Dam, the Canso Causeway, the harnessing of the Nelson and Churchill Rivers, are relatively small scale examples of what the future could hold." It is essential that as a nation we try to determine what this really means to the future of Canada.

It has long been an academic parlour game to try to define the "Canadian identity", usually with remarkable lack of success. Inevitably, when indulged in publicly through television or radio, the exercise induces acute boredom in the audience and the participating intellectuals conclude that there is no such definable thing. But the late Blair Fraser, who through much of his distinguished journalistic career tried to capture the meaning of Canada, put it this way:

"Development" continues. Canada's standard of living, second highest in the world ... is in no danger of losing that proud position. Washing machines and television sets abound ... superhighways devour uncounted acres of fertile land, and the second highest incidence of automobiles achieves, in the metropolitan areas, the second highest air pollution. Ugly little towns prosper, all calling themselves cities and all looking like faithful copies of Omaha, Nebraska. This is not a Canada to call forth any man's love. But just north of it lies a different kind of land — too barren ever to be thickly settled, too bleak to be popular like Blackpool or Miami. There is no reason to doubt that it will always be there, and so long as it is there Canada will not die.

Blair Fraser died canoeing in the white water that he loved. There seems reason to believe that he was closer than most to defining the Canadian identity, that it is indeed something closely associated with the land itself, and with the integrity of that land. He was not alone in finding something essential to Canada in the wilderness. Fred Bodsworth has pointed out:

It is no coincidence that our national emblem is not a rising sun, a star, a hammer, a sickle, or a dragon, but a beaver and a maple leaf. Nor is it coincidence that there are more paintings of wilderness lakes, spruce bogs, and pine trees on more Canadian living room walls than in any other nation on earth. We may scoff, we may deny, but the wilderness mystique is still a strong element of the Canadian ethos.

The strength of a nation lies not in cost benefit ratios, but in the sense its citizens have of what it is. For most, these deeper realities defy expression. It is the business of the writer and other artists to search them out. Northrop Frye, perhaps our greatest critic, says: "Everything that is central in Canadian writing seems to be marked by the immanence of the natural world."

That natural landscape is integrally linked with and dependent upon free flowing rivers. So perhaps some of the essence of Canada is to be found in the Albany River in Northern Ontario, the South Saskatchewan River as it carves its way through Medicine Hat, in the Nahanni as it leaps and crashes over Virginia Falls, in fishermen netting salmon at the mouth of the Fraser River, in Cree Indian Communities along the Rupert River in Quebec, in the small farms and big mountains along the Columbia and Kootenay Rivers of the Rocky Mountain Trench, in the tundra that stretches to the Arctic Ocean, nourished and drained by the MacKenzie River. It must have something to do with the fields of grain that ripple and ripen on the plains of Saskatchewan, divided by the spectacular Qu'Appelle Valley, or with the way the granite of the Canadian Shield drops into the water of Lake Athabasca, giving way to endless level stretches of river and lake and muskeg and stunted northern trees.

These, and many more regions of Canada, have been or may be much changed by water development. For the land of Canada, and the water that helped create it, that drains, waters, and in so many ways maintains it, are indivisible. Where land and water are most closely associated we seek our recreation, we build our cities, we find greatest beauty, we centre our commerce. At the union between land and water we find the best of Canada. And it is here that the greatest destruction, both planned and unplanned, occurs when natural water courses are manipulated.

So much of Canada is involved in water development that we must recognize that we are building toward a Canada that will have few salmon fishermen, where the independent farms of the naturally watered valleys will be replaced by the highly subsidized irrigation farmers spawned by the large prairie water projects. Those Indians of Canada who have maintained their life on the land will be gone and with the disappearance of that way of life will fade a vital part of the fabric of the nation. The possibility of dispersing populations away from the metropolitan areas of the country will be largely foregone as the valleys that would be most hospitable for settlement disappear under water. Politically this perhaps is not very persuasive because developments occurring at any one time are widely separated, there are not usually large numbers of people involved in each project, and the total national impact of all projects is not publicly recognized.

Generally, those people displaced are Canadians whose

roots go deep in the land — centuries in the case of our native Indians, often for more than a generation in the case of non-Indians. There are those who think that ways of life such as these are doomed anyway, and that flooding such people out is simply hurrying along an inevitable process. This is the thesis of a study of the flooding of Southern Indian Lake conducted by Van Ginkel Associates and Hedlin Menzies and Associates of Winnipeg. It is a view that most Canadians have probably shared during much of the postwar period, but it is an attitude which is rapidly becoming displaced by the recognition that the mainstream of technological, urbanized society is perhaps not the mold into which everyone should be forced regardless of his wishes. The rather arrogant assumption that it is the only viable way of life is seriously questioned by Canadians of all ages and races.

To base public policy of such a far reaching and permanent nature as water development on a philosophy that is very much in a state of change is indefensible. No one can predict whether future Canadians will wish to make use of opportunities to choose from a wide variety of life styles. But it surely is questionable whether the present generation of Canadians has the right to foreclose such options forever by destroying the land and water base that makes such choices possible.

Even if the reasoning underlying manipulation of people as a result of water development were accepted as legitimate, it must be asked how many people can be sacrificed "for the common good". For the cumulative total of human pain and dislocation and foregone opportunities caused by water development is becoming very large, though it is still far below what can be expected if present plans get off the drawing boards. At what point does the cost of sacrificing so much and so many to "the good of the majority" become too great a price to pay? We will never answer this question as long as we look at water development one project at a time.

The *total* impact of water development is seldom considered in Canada. But it is clear that one powerful effect of it is to speed the homogenization of the nation, forcing its people into a common mold by eliminating the land and resources that foster independence and freedom of choice, and subsidizing metropolitan growth and industrialization by means of artificially cheap power and water. With every dam, there dies further opportunity for the diversity of life that has been an essential part of Canada. With the disappearance of these uniquely Canadian attributes, this country will differ little in fact or philosophy from the rest of North America.

So water development, whether initially for export or not, has to be a key issue in any consideration of Canadian independence. Water export would result in the creation of permanent physical ties with the United States, and in increasingly complex political and administrative structures linking our two countries. Or, great water developments might be undertaken in large measure to export electric power, as in the case of current Quebec and Manitoba projects. Since it was spelled out by the Honorable Mitchell Sharp in 1963, an important part of Canadian energy policy "would permit the export of large blocks of power to the United States for a relatively long period of years to assist in the immediate development of certain large scale Canadian power projects, particularly undeveloped hydro resources which might not be viable in the near future unless provision were made for the marketing in the United States of a significant portion of their output." Since this statement was made prior to the really large hydro projects of recent years and before the ramifications of such water developments became clear, it was perhaps reasonable for the time. Subsequent developments and increased understanding of the consequences of water development clearly indicate the need for reassessment of this policy.

Hydro developments that export power to the United States will earn American money to help pay for the actual facilities, but will return nothing in compensation for the despoliation of vast areas of Canadian landscape and the foregone opportunities for Canadians that this loss represents. As Professor Cass Booy, former Chairman of the Manitoba Water Resources Commission, puts it: "We throw in the natural resources, the water resources of our province and we give up our wild rivers, our rapids and our beautiful falls, we allow the spoiling of our beaches and our lake fronts, we change and upset the ecological balance over vast areas and in that way we actually impoverish our people for the purpose of this demand." In exporting hydro-electric energy, we are in effect exporting some of the best of Canada. And we are giving it away at no cost to the American consumer of that energy.

Bruce Hutchinson, having made his journalistic recognition of the attitudes of the day, concluded his book *The Fraser* with what one is led to feel are the real feelings of this man who has probably thought about and loved Canada as deeply as anyone of his generation.

How fast the time has gone! How little of the river life that we knew in our boyhood, yesterday! All crushed beneath the marching boot of progress, improved beyond recognition, civilized in shape and spirit alien to us ... For us it is enough that we knew the days before the engineers came ... Enough that we lived upon these banks, looked down at the moving water, felt the motion of blind force, sensed the substance of a continent, and caught a glimpse of the reality of the earth, which it is the chief business of man's society to disguise ... We have had the best of it. We have seen the river, naked and virginal, when we were young.

But where Hutchinson accepted, sadly it seems, the inevitability of the damming and manipulation of his Fraser, now, almost a quarter of a century later, growing numbers of Canadians seem doubtful of the wisdom that would allow the current trend of massive water development to continue without question. There is less willingness to allow such feeling to be written off as impractical emotionalism. Why should Hutchinson's be the last generation to have known a wild river, to have "caught a glimpse of the reality of the earth?"

Losses that recently were accepted as a necessary part of the price of progress may now be considered of greater value and significance to the nation than they once were. Is it possible that this surfacing uneasiness may be deeply rooted in the identity of Canada? What, for example, does all this mean to a Torontonian, or a Winnipegger, or any of the millions of Canadians, who will not personally be directly affected by water development? They may of course make use of the rivers and lakes of their country for recreation, and the quality of that experience will diminish as more people make greater use of a resource that is being reduced in quantity and quality.

But beyond that, we must ask to what extent it is possible to eliminate the basis on which to a considerable extent rests the *idea* of Canada, without damaging the nation itself. We have seen how central the free flowing water of Canada is to the conception of their nation held by Canadians. With the continuation of present water development patterns, it will at some point become clear to Canadians that the Canada they believed in no longer exists, that the best of it has been sacrificed in a few decades of dam building. What will happen to the spirit of the nation, its will to live, when it becomes clear that it merely exists as a political entity, that only lines on a map designate Canada as a separate and distinctive nation?

The question of Canada's survival as a nation sharing a common border with the United States has long been a contentious issue in this country. The extent of political and economic control of Canada by the United States, and this nation's sensitivity to every action of its great neighbour are facts of Canadian life. And as the ownership of Canadian commerce and industry becomes even further concentrated in American hands with the eager assistance of the governments and banks of Canada, Canada's independence becomes to a growing extent a fondly-regarded but fading myth.

Many avenues of varying merit are proposed to slow and reverse the trend toward American absorption of Canada. It has been suggested that soon this country will soon be almost totally dominated by American decision making, without having a vote in that process — a classic definition of a colony. The federal government has put forth as its answer a process that would screen any proposed foreign take-overs of Canadian companies; few apart from official government spokesmen expect such a law to accomplish much. The New Democratic Party, the Committee for an Independent Canada, and many individuals in and out of all political parties, have called for much more severe restrictions ensuring for Canadians ownership and control of their own nation.

But surely all such proposals miss the central point, the essence of which has been stated by Canadian philosopher George Grant: "Canada could only continue to be if we could hold some alternative social vision to that of the great republic."

The direction in which the United States is leading Canada and much of the western world has been ably analyzed by such scholars as French Sociologist Jacques Ellul in *The Technological Society*, and by American author Lewis Mumford in a series of books culminating in *The Pentagon of Power*. The imperatives of technology and efficiency, progress and growth, have so dominated Western thinking that few objections are raised when men are termed "human resources," to be considered as factors of production along with resources from field and sea and rock. In Mumford's words, Western man has put himself in the service of "a purely mechanical system whose processes can neither be retarded nor redirected nor halted, that has no internal mechanism for warning of defects or correcting them, and that can only be accelerated [and which] is, as we have all too late found out, a menace to mankind."

The cost in environmental destruction of such a system is all too evident in the United States and in many parts of Canada. "The technology which has enabled the United States to put a man on the moon has also given us the capability of threatening the very base of our existence on this beautiful but fragile planet." The social impact of the system in terms of alienation, and mental illness is increasingly documented and publicised. "The age of affluence, technological marvels, and medical miracles is paradoxically the age of chronic ailments, of anxiety, and even of despair... Alienation is generated, furthermore, by the complete failure of even the most affluent societies to achieve harmonious relationships between human life and the total environment." This lack of harmony between man and nature is seen at perhaps its most extreme in North American water development programs and proposals.

It has become very clear that unending growth of populations, economies, technology, and production for its own sake is impossible. It must eventually level off or result in disintegration of the system. This inevitability has been documented by biologists and earth scientists for several years, and in 1972 was spelled out in a popular way in *The Limits to Growth* by Dennis Meadows, et al., of the Massachusetts Institute of Technology. It has become particularly evident that the longer a nation delays contending with the inevitability of an end to rapid growth and development the more difficult the job will become with each year. Rates of growth will be ever greater in absolute terms, and the problems of slowing and governing and re-directing the economy will be closer to an impossibility. This is why many observers suggest that Canada can still choose, while population growth and pollution and resource depletion are at manageable levels.

It is fascinating, if horrifying, to observe the truth of

Mumford's statement of the basic impossibility of correcting or slowing or in any way guiding a system which is so evidently on a course of self-destructiveness. Whatever ills beset our nation, the only solutions that are forthcoming from the capitals of Canada describe means to drive the system even faster, to cure the ills of technology by still more technological innovation, to solve the problems of a society burdened by overrapid growth with still greater and faster economic growth.

Of course, technology carefully selected for its benefits to mankind, and growth where it can clearly improve the welfare and dignity of human beings, should occur. But these are not the criteria by which growth and technology are applied in our society. If we *can* go to the moon, drill an oil well on a remote arctic island, dam a great river, build a freeway or a sixty-storey highrise, it is part of growth and progress, and it proceeds. If we *can* create a market for a product, no matter how useless, we produce it regardless of environmental or social cost. If a provincial government can obtain American money to "develop" (meaning "deplete") a natural resource, it will do so with no consideration of the effect of delivering still more of the nation into foreign hands. There is no selectivity for human well-being in the growth and progress of our technological western society. Dr. Donald Chant of the University of Toronto has insisted that we must reject the "can-should" equation; the mere fact that we are able to do something does not necessarily mean we *should* do it.

Water development, whether for export of water or energy, or for use in Canada, is a prime example of this technological imperative. In the United States, we have seen how agencies and institutions proceed with water development for its own sake at great cost to social and natural systems in that country. We can see that Canada has shown every sign of adopting without change the same pattern of development of water resources. Alberta's PRIME program, the Saskatchewan-Nelson Basin Study, the Churchill Nelson Hydro scheme in Manitoba, the Columbia Treaty dams, the James Bay Scheme in Quebec, the Mactaquac dam on the Saint John River in New Brunswick, are all developments in the classic American tradition.

If a decision is made to export Canadian water to the United States, the physical, economic and political ties will be immediate and obvious. The movement south of the last resource that Canadians still own will mark the total dedication of the resources and life of our nation to the ever more rapid and suicidal growth of the U.S. economy. If on the other hand major water development proceeds along its present path in Canada it will, as we have described in the scenario in chapter 5, likely lead eventually to major export schemes anyway, as the pieces fall into place. But even if no drop of water ever flows across the border as a result of Canadian water development, the longer term effect on the nation of such schemes will likely be the same as deliberate export policies. The dedication of our most precious natural resource to the march of the technological juggernaut will be an enormous step in tying Canada to the imperatives of the American technological empire. The destruction of a river and the land with which it is interdependent, and the elimination of the social structures that were indigenous to it, are irreversible steps locking the country into a future that it has not consciously chosen.

We have seen how major water development is perhaps the greatest possible step toward elimination of the diversification of life and land that makes Canada the fascinating nation that it is. It is perhaps the type of technological "progress" that leads most directly to the removal of the choices for Canadians that this diversity represents. We must not forget that the availability of options — a wide range of available choices in life-style and environment — is an essential part of individual freedom. "The assumption that progress is necessarily headed in a good or benevolent direction becomes more and more clearly an unjustified assumption," writes Northrop Frye in *The Modern Century*. "For most thoughtful people progress has lost most of its original sense of a favourable value-judgment and has become simply progression, toward a goal more likely to be a disaster than an improvement." Water development in Canada is a classic example of progress as Frye has described it.

A deliberate choice by Canadians that their country will reject current technological imperatives and choose instead to emphasize those factors leading to diversity and a wide range of choice for Canadians, may be the first step toward the "alternative social vision" that George Grant suggests is necessary for the nation's survival. Total rejection of the current mania for damming and diverting almost every free flowing river in the nation would be an enormous step in that direction. It would also be a vital move toward the creation of a nation that is prepared to live within the limits of nature before being forced to do so by an exhausted and polluted environment.

For there is no question at all that Canadians must come to terms with the limits of their resources at some stage. Fortunate as this nation is, it is not infinite in its material resources or in the ability of its environment to absorb insult and injury. The only real question is when this reconciliation will take place — now, while a chance of an independent existence in a livable environment still remains; or later, when with Canada as an integral part of the American economic and technological system, a demeaned and depleted North America is forced to face the consequences of total "development" and ever faster "growth". Canada's water policy decisions will be a crucial element in the choice of an alternative future, and therefore in the survival of this nation.

Notes on sources and references
Interviews

In the preparation of this book, scores of academic papers on the subject were studied, too many to list here. The most influential are acknowledged in the introduction. Excellent material was also found in *The Atlantic Monthly*, *Maclean's Magazine* and *The Saturday Review*, and in the *Christian Science Monitor*, the *Financial Post*, the *New York Times*, the Toronto *Globe and Mail* and the *Vancouver Sun*.

Much research for the book, and for the earlier CBC film of the same name, was carried out by means of personal interviews with people concerned about water resources across Canada and the United States during 1970 and 1971. In the introduction, some people who were particularly influential in shaping what became the basic philosophy of the book are mentioned. Many others contributed greatly to providing a breadth of fact and understanding that was essential to the project. Following is a list, in alphabetical order, of some of those with whom interviews were held in preparing this book:

Carl Bevins, President, Imperial Irrigation District, El Centro, California.

Kenneth Boulding, University of Colorado, Boulder, Colorado.

Cass Booy, University of Manitoba, Winnipeg, Manitoba.

David Brower, President, Friends of the Earth, San Francisco, California.

Stewart Brandberg, Executive Director, The Wilderness Society, Washington, D.C.

David Cass-Beggs, Chairman, Manitoba Hydro, Winnipeg, Manitoba.

Donald Chant, University of Toronto, Toronto, Ontario.

Gerald Cole, Arizona State University, Scotsdale, Arizona.

James A. Crutchfield, University of Washington, Seattle, Washington.

Donald Currie, Alberta Research Council, Edmonton, Alberta.

Kenneth Dawson, Lakehead University, Thunder Bay, Ontario.

T. C. Douglas, former leader, New Democratic Party, Ottawa, Ontario.

Paul Ehrlich, Stanford University, Palo Alto, California.

William Gianelli, Director, Dept. of Water Resources, State of California, Sacramento, California.

Michael Goldberg, University of British Columbia, Vancouver, B.C.

Joe Greene, former Minister of Mines, Energy and Resources, Ottawa, Ontario.

John Hare, President, Canadian Water Resources Association, Winnipeg, Manitoba.

Larratt Higgins, Economist, Ontario Hydro, Toronto, Ontario.

John Holdren, California Institute of Technology, Pasadena, California.

C. S. Holling, University of British Columbia, Vancouver, B.C.

Charles Howe, Resources for the Future, Inc., Washington, D.C.

Henry Jackson, U.S. Senator, State of Washington.

Joseph Jensen, Chairman, Metropolitan Water District of Southern California, Los Angeles, California.

Rich Johnson, The Central Arizona Project Association, Phoenix, Arizona.

Roland P. Kelly, Vice-President, The Ralph M. Parsons Engineering Company, Los Angeles, California.

Fred Knelman, Sir George Williams University, Montreal, Quebec.

John V. Krutilla, Resources For the Future, Inc., Washington, D.C.

E. Kuiper, University of Manitoba, Winnipeg, Manitoba.

Arleigh Laycock, University of Alberta, Edmonton, Alberta.

Luna B. Leopold, U.S. Geological Service, Washington, D.C.

Starker Leopold, University of California, Berkeley, California.

Daniel Luten, University of California, Berkeley, California.

Tom McCall, Governor, State of Oregon.

Dennis McDonald, Regional Fisheries Biologist, Calgary, Alberta.

William Martin, University of Arizona, Tucson, Arizona.

Grant Mitchell, Executive Director, Saskatchewan Water Resources Commission, Regina, Saskatchewan.

Frank Moss, U.S. Senator, State of Utah.

Gordon Nelson, University of Calgary, Calgary, Alberta.

Robert Newbury, University of Manitoba, Winnipeg, Manitoba.

Senor Ojeda, Manager, Water Supply System, Tijuana, Mexico.

Arthur Pilsbury, University of California, Los Angeles.

A. T. Prince, Department of the Environment, Ottawa, Ontario.

Frank Quinn, Department of the Environment, Ottawa, Ontario.

Sol Resnick, University of Arizona, Tucson, Arizona.

David Seckler, University of California, Berkeley, California.

Senior Officials of the Santee, California, Water System.

W. R. Derrick Sewell, University of Victoria, Victoria, B.C.

Henry Shipley, Asst. General Manager, Salt River Project, Phoenix, Arizona.

Lewis Gordy Smith, Water Resources Engineer, Denver, Colorado.

Stewart Smith, Environment Conservation Authority, Government of Alberta, Edmonton, Alberta.

Peggy Spaw, Arizona Conservation Council, Phoenix, Arizona.

John Spence, McGill University, Montreal, Quebec.

Robert Stanfield, Leader, Progressive Conservative Party, Ottawa.

Harry Strom, former Premier, Province of Alberta.

Buzz Taisey, Resort Operator, Orient Bay, Ontario.

E. Roy Tinney, Department of the Environment, Ottawa, Ontario.

Dixon Thompson, Science Council of Canada, Ottawa, Ontario.

Joseph Tofanni, U.S. Army Corps of Engineers, Washington, D.C.

Jerome Waldie, U.S. Congressman, California.

Gilbert White, University of Colorado, Boulder, Colorado.

Jack Williams, Governor, State of Arizona.

Richard Wilson, Rancher, Round Valley, California.

Reports

These are the more important published reports referred to in the preparation of the book:

Chapin D. Clark, "Northwest-Southwest Water Diversion", *Willamette Law Journal*, Fall 1965.

Daedalus, The Journal of the American Academy of Arts and Sciences, Fall 1967.

"Death of a Delta", a statement issued in 1970 by 16 Alberta Scientists concerning the danger to the Peace-Athabaska Delta resulting from the Bennett Dam in British Columbia.

"Environment 1975", a Symposium sponsored by the Biological Sciences Society, The University of Calgary, February, 1970, edited by D. A. Brookes and M. T. Myres.

"Fisheries Problems Related to Moran Dam on the Fraser River", prepared by Technical Staffs of the Canadian Department of the Environment, and the International Pacific Salmon Fisheries Commission, Vancouver, B.C., August, 1971.

"NAWAPA—North American Water and Power Alliance", The Ralph M. Parsons Company, Los Angeles, 1966.

"Nawapa: A Continental Water System", *Bulletin of the Atomic Scientists*, September, 1967.

"Oregon's Long Range Requirements For Water", State Water Resources Board, Salem, Oregon, 1969.

"Power and Land in California", Robert C. Fellmeth, Editor, Center For Study of Responsive Law, Washington, D.C.

"A Preliminary Study of the Environmental Impacts of the James Bay Development Project, Quebec", The Report of the Joint Federal-Provincial Task Force, December, 1971.

"Proceedings of the Columbia River Water Congress", Wenatchee, Washington, April, 1966.

"Proceedings of the Peace-Athabaska Delta Symposium", The University of Alberta, Edmonton, January, 1971.

Frank J. Quinn, *Area of Origin Protectionism in Western States*, A Doctoral Dissertation for the University of Washington, Seattle, 1970.

W. R. Derrick Sewell, and Ian Burton, Editors, *Perceptions and Attitudes in Resources Management*, Policy Research and Coordination Branch, Department of Energy, Mines and Resources, Ottawa.

"Transition in the North—The Churchill River Diversion and the People of South Indian Lake", a study prepared for the Manitoba Development Authority by Van Ginkel Associates, in association with Hedlin, Menzies and Associates Ltd., Winnipeg, 1967.

"Water and Survival—a Study of the Relationship of Water Development to the Identity of Canada," by Richard C. Bocking, Agassiz Centre For Water Studies, University of Manitoba, Winnipeg, 1972.

"Water Diversion Proposals of North America", a report prepared for the Canadian Council of Resource Ministers, by the Water Resources Division of the Alberta Government, 1968.

"Western Water Development—A Summary of Water Resources Projects, Plans, and Studies Relating to the Western and Midwestern United States". Compiled by the Special Subcommittee on Western Water Development of the Committee on Public Works, United States Senate, Washington, 1966.

Selected bibliography

J. M. Bagley and T. L. Smiley, Editors, Water Importation Into Arid Lands, a Symposium of the American Association for the Advancement of Science, Dallas, Texas, 1968, in *Arid Lands in Perspective*, The University of Arizona Press, Tucson.

Marston Bates, *The Forest and the Sea*, Random House Inc., New York, 1960.

R. H. Boyle, J. Graves and T. H. Watkins, *The Water Hustlers*, The Sierra Club, San Francisco, 1971.

M. J. Campbell, *The Saskatchewan*, Holt Rinehart and Winston, Inc., Toronto, 1950.

A. H. Carhart, *Water—or Your Life*, J. B. Lippincott Co., Philadelphia, 1951.

J. S. Cram, *Water, Canadian Needs and Resources,* Harvest House Ltd., Montreal, 1968.

Donald Creighton, *Canada's First Century*, The Macmillan Company of Canada Ltd., Toronto, 1970.

F. F. Darling and J. P. Milton, *Future Environments of North America*, The Natural History Press, New York, 1966.

Ian E. Efford and Barbara M. Smith, Editors, *Energy and the Environment*, Institute of Resource Ecology, University of British Columbia, 1972.

Roderick L. Haig-Brown, *A River Never Sleeps*, William Morrow and Company, New York, 1946.

Jack Hirshleifer, J. C. DeHaven and J. W. Milliman, *Water Supply Economics, Technology and Policy*, The University of Chicago Press, Chicago, 1960.

C. W. Howe and K. W. Easter, *Interbasin Transfers of Water: Economic Issues and Impacts*, The Johns Hopkins Press, Baltimore, 1971.

Bruce Hutchinson, *The Fraser*, Holt Rinehart and Winston, Inc., and Clarke, Irwin and Company Ltd., Toronto, 1950.

H. B. N. Hynes, *The Ecology of Running Waters*, The University of Toronto Press, Toronto, 1970.

Harold A. Innis, *The Fur Trade in Canada*, revised edition, University of Toronto Press, Toronto, 1970.

John V. Krutilla, *The Columbia River Treaty*, The Johns Hopkins Press, Baltimore, 1967.

Karl F. Lagler, "Ecological Effects of Hydroelectric Dams", from *Power Generation and Environmental Change*, Edited by David A. Berkowitz and Arthur M. Squires, from the Symposium of the Committee on Environmental Alteration, the American Association for the Advancement of Science, The MIT Press, Cambridge, 1971.

James Laxer, *The Politics of the Continental Resources Deal*, New Press, Toronto, 1970.

Russell Lord, *The Care of the Earth*, Thomas Nelson and Sons, New York, 1962.

J. W. MacNeil, *Environmental Management*, Information Canada, Ottawa, 1971.

E. J. Mishan, *The Costs of Economic Growth*, Penguin Books, Harmondsworth, England, 1969.

Eric W. Morse, *Fur Trade Routes of Canada*, The Queens's Printer, Ottawa, 1969.

Frank E. Moss, *The Water Crisis*, Praeger Publishers, New York, 1967.

National Academy of Sciences, National Research Council, *Alternatives in Water Management*, National Academy of Sciences, Washington, 1966.

National Academy of Sciences, National Research Council, *Water and Choice in the Colorado Basin*, National Academy of Sciences, Washington, 1968.

J. G. Nelson and M. J. Chambers, Editors, *Water*, Methuen Publications, Toronto, 1969.

D. H. Pimlott, C. J. Kerswill and J. R. Bider, *Scientific Activities in Fisheries and Wildlife Resources*, Special Background Study No. 15 for the Science Council of Canada, Information Canada, Ottawa, 1971.

R. E. Richardson, W. G. Rooke and G. H. McNevin, *Developing Water Resources*, The Ryerson Press and MacLean-Hunter Limited, Toronto, 1969.

W. R. Derrick Sewell, *Water Management and Floods in the Fraser River Basin*, University of Chicago Press, Chicago, 1965.

Borden Spears, Editor, *Wilderness Canada*, Clarke, Irwin and Company Ltd., Toronto, 1970.

John Swettenham, *McNaughton* (Vol. 3), The Ryerson Press, Toronto, 1969.

Donald Waterfield, *Continental Waterboy*, Clarke, Irwin and Company, Ltd., Toronto, 1970.

T. H. Watkins et al, *The Grand Colorado*, American West Publishing Company, Palo Alto, 1969.

United States Water Resources Council, *The Nation's Water Resources*, Superintendant of Documents, Washington, 1968.

Selected subject index

Also from James Lewis & Samuel . . .

Quebec: A Chronicle 1968-1972
An account of five crucial years in Quebec's history which records the events of October 1970 and the emergence of the labour movements as a major political force. Paper $1.95.

Corporate Canada
Fourteen articles on major Canadian corporations like Eaton's, branch-plant industries like computers, and major economic policy issues like regional incentives grants and energy, drawn from the pages of Last Post magazine. Paper $1.95.

Louder Voices: The Corporate Welfare Bums
David Lewis puts together the information about what he calls the corporate welfare system, in a book which will be of interest to Canadians as long as government policies and the tax system remain unchanged. Paper $1.95.

Read Canadian
A book which introduces Canadian books in more than thirty areas, from urban problems to the history of the West. Paper $1.95.

Up Against City Hall
Toronto's most controversial alderman, John Sewell, reports on his attempts to win victories for citizens' groups and to reduce the power of the land development industry at city hall. Paper $2.95.

She Named It Canada
A witty, entertaining, attractive illustrated history of Canada written by the Corrective Collective, a Vancouver-based women's group. Paper $1.00.

A History of Canadian Wealth
Gustavus Myers' classic of Canadian economic and
political history-writing, exposing our own home-grown
robber barons and con-men, the wheelers and dealers in
land and votes and lives. Written in 1913 and never before
published in Canada, Myers' book has been acclaimed.
Paper $2.95.

Quebec in Question
A short, lucid separatist's history of Quebec written by
sociologist Marcel Rioux and translated by James Boake.
Paper $3.50.

The Citizens' Guide to City Politics
The first practical and realistic guide to how city hall
operates and why, which focusses on the links between
city government and the real estate and land development
industry. Written by James Lorimer. Paper $3.95.

An Unauthorized History of the RCMP
The Browns recount the role of the RCMP in Canadian
history — in the Winnipeg General Strike and other labour
disturbances in 1919, in intelligence work and infiltration
of the Canadian Communist Party, in strikebreaking
in the late 1920s and early 1930s, in persecuting
immigrants and radicals during the Depression, in waging
war on the unemployed during the 30's, in intelligence
during the Second World War, and in dealing with
students, draft dodgers and farmers during the 60s.
Paper. $1.95.

Working People
Life in a downtown city neighbourhood by James Lorimer
and Myfanwy Phillips.
    The first account to be published in Canada of the life
of working-class Canadians. First published in 1971,
Working People has made for itself a reputation both
as social science and as a literary achievement. Paper $4.95.

The Real World of City Politics
Six case studies of Toronto city politics which define
the realities of civic government in Canada and show how
these realities are being challenged by citizen groups. $2.95.